Rite Aid
GUIDE TO HEALTH

Anti-Aging

*Secrets to Help You
Slow Down the Aging Process*

Donald Vaughn

Published by
Adams Media, an F+W Publications Company
57 Littlefield Street
Avon, MA 02322
www.adamsmedia.com

ISBN 10: 1-59337-697-9
ISBN 13: 978-1-59337-697-0

Printed in Canada.

J I H G F E D C B

Library of Congress Cataloging-in-Publication Data
available from the publisher.

This book includes material from *The Everything® Anti-Aging Book* by Donald
Vaughn, ©2002, F+W Publications, Inc.

Rite Aid Guide to Health: Anti-Aging is intended as a reference volume only,
not as a medical manual. In light of the complex, individual, and specific
nature of heath problems, this book is not intended to replace professional
medical advice. The ideas, procedures, and suggestions in this book are
intended to supplement, not replace, the advice of a trained medical professional. Consult your physician before adopting the suggestions in this book.
The author and publisher disclaim any liability arising directly or indirectly
from the use of this book.

This publication is designed to provide accurate and authoritative information with regard to the subject matter covered. It is sold with the understanding that the publisher is not engaged in rendering legal, accounting, or other
professional advice. If legal advice or other expert assistance is required, the
services of a competent professional person should be sought.

—From a *Declaration of Principles* jointly adopted by a Committee of the
American Bar Association and a Committee of Publishers and Associations

Many of the designations used by manufacturers and sellers to distinguish
their product are claimed as trademarks. Where those designations appear in
this book and Adams Media was aware of a trademark claim, the designations
have been printed with initial capital letters.

Contents

Introduction   ix

Chapter 1   1
Starting Out Right

The Quest for Immortality   2

Working with Your Doctor   5

Lifetime Checkups   12

Customizing Your Personal   14
Anti-Aging Plan

Chapter 2   19
The Lowdown on Aging

The Physiology of Aging   20

The Psychological Effects of Aging   26

The Emotional Effects of Aging   27

Maintaining Mental Acuity   29

Chapter 3   35
Exercise and Nutrition

The Importance of Exercise   36

The Role of Nutrition   39

Good Foods versus Bad Foods   40

Vitamins and Minerals   42

Chapter 4   53
Herbal Remedies

Herbs and Your Anti-Aging Regimen   54

Testing the Medical Use of Herbs   55

Playing It Safe   58

Herbs for Common Ailments   63

Chapter 5   69
Anti-Aging Tactics

The Effects of Stress on Health and Aging   70

Stress Reduction Made Easy   72

Beating the Blues   75

Sex and Longevity   78

Chapter 6   85
Age-Related Diseases

Common Diseases and Conditions of Aging   86

The Role of Genetics and Family History   95

Prevention of Aging Diseases   97

Chapter 7   101
Take a Look Around

Longevity and Your Environment   102

Common Environmental Hazards   103

Water Pollution   106

Air Pollution   109

Chapter 8   117
Social Support Systems

How Social Support Keeps Us Healthy   118

The Role of Family   119

The Role of Friends   122

Charity and Volunteerism: 126
The Importance of Community
Involvement

Social Support in Old Age   127

Chapter 9   133
Specifics for Individual Populations

Recognizing Differences   134

Anti-Aging and Men   136

Anti-Aging and Women   143

Nutrition for Women   146

Women and Anti-Aging Supplementation   151

Pregnancy and Childbearing: 153
How It Can Affect Your Aging

Anti-Aging and the Senior Population   154

Adhering Your Lifestyle to Your Age   158

Anti-Aging and the Differently Abled   161

Chapter 10   **165**
Stay Informed

The Antioxidant Approach   166

The Caloric Restriction Approach   169

The Natural Hormone Approach   173

The Mineral Approach   187

Appendix A 199
More Sources of Information

Appendix B 203
Organizations and Associations

Index 210

Introduction

For all of us, aging is an inevitable part of life. However, the thought of us aging shouldn't make us cringe. If we take a proactive approach to developing an anti-aging regimen grounded in nutrition, exercise, and healthful living, we can embrace our later years as some of the best years of our lives. We don't have to wait fur future science to slow the aging process—there's plenty we can do right now to hedge our bet against Father Time.

How well we age, and ultimately, how long we live have as much, if not more, to do with the many lifestyle choices we make every day as with our genetic background, risk of chronic illness, or any number of uncontrollable factors. Bottom line: It really is possible to age well if you're willing to work at it.

Chapter 1

Starting Out Right

Benjamin Franklin noted that the only certainties in life are death and taxes. Most doctors would probably agree that old Ben was wrong; a third certainty faces us all—and that is aging. Indeed, aging is an inescapable part of being alive. From conception to death, the aging process slowly, perniciously affects our bodies and our minds. You can fight it but you can't stop it.

The Quest for Immortality

For most of us, the realization that we're growing older doesn't really sink in until the first sign of gray hair and wrinkles. Only then do thoughts of our own mortality become increasingly common.

Age plays a vital role in the development of disease. Though infection and a handful of childhood disorders are more common in young people, most degenerative diseases afflict people over forty. This includes Alzheimer's disease, most forms of cancer, osteoporosis, heart disease, non-insulin-dependent diabetes, stroke, and osteoarthritis. These and many other diseases are triggered by advancing age—which is one of the most important reasons for researchers to strive to better understand the aging process.

Until very recently, there wasn't much we could do to hold at bay the aging process aside from exercise and a healthy diet. Over the past two decades, however, researchers have made astounding advances in their understanding of aging and what can be done to slow it down. Researchers know more now than ever before about the importance of proper nutrition;

replacement body parts are being successfully grown in the laboratory; and the international Human Genome Project promises to help eliminate or cure a wide variety of conditions that in the past cut life short, or made growing older a painful burden.

Prehistoric people were lucky if they lived to be twenty; however, children born today, researchers say, can expect to live well into their seventies, eighties, and beyond in relatively good health.

And what will the future hold? The prospects are unbelievable. Some futurists believe that if science continues its current pace, man will one day live 130, 140, even 150 years. At the moment, 120 years is considered the absolute limit of human longevity. It's impossible, scientists say, for the human machine to function longer than that, no matter how healthful our lifestyle. But in the minds of many age specialists, a 120-year lifespan is a barrier that can and will be broken.

Current and future breakthroughs in the science of aging promise to raise some moral and ethical questions. Would we *want* to live to 150?

What quality of life could people expect? What burdens would this place on society in regard to health care, population, and so forth? What are the emotional and psychological implications of extreme longevity? Where do we draw the line? In theory, nutrition supplementation, gene therapy, laboratory organ growth/natural regeneration, and approaches that are now only in the conceptual stage could one day give us humans capable of living not decades but centuries.

We know that there is no Fountain of Youth, no elixir or pill that will erase the signs and symptoms of age. However, there are many ways to slow the aging process and, in some situations, to reverse it. For example, many of us can extend our life span by making a few lifestyle changes, such as eating less red meat and more vegetables, exercising, and not smoking.

It's important that anti-aging not be approached in a haphazard manner. To age well and stay young, it's necessary to formulate an anti-aging regimen that improves every aspect of your physical and mental well-being every day. Tips for such a regimen can be found throughout this book.

It's important that you work with your doctor in formulating and maintaining your anti-aging regimen. No one knows more about your health than your personal physician, and his or her input can go a long way toward creating the game plan that addresses your specific needs and goals.

Throughout this book, we'll examine how and why the body ages, what factors influence our rate and degree of aging, and what we can do to stay as young as possible for as long as possible. Always remember, however: No matter how long you live, life is still short. Enjoy it while you can.

Working with Your Doctor

Selecting a doctor is one of the most important decisions you can make when it comes to your health. When choosing a doctor, it's important that you do your homework and ask questions before making your decision.

Finding Common Ground

One of the most important considerations is how attuned your physician is to you, your needs, and your goals. In addition to your primary health care, it's essential that your doctor understand how important it is to you to live as many good years as you possibly can. Many so-called "old-school" doctors disagree with the holistic approach to medicine and don't value the desire to incorporate health, nutrition, and breaking advances in science and medicine to help you live longer. These physicians prefer instead to treat your problem and send you on your way.

Compatibility is essential in fostering a good relationship with your physician. Hopefully, you will be working closely not only in maintaining your health but also in designing the anti-aging regimen that is best for you.

Your doctor should be well versed in the importance of nutrition, exercise, lifestyle, and science in adding years to your life and life to your years. Ideally, the two of you will share responsibility for a common goal: helping you live as long as you possibly can.

One would think that all doctors would share this vision, but such is not the case. Many doctors are lucky if they get to spend ten minutes with each patient. Under such constraints, it's all they can do to evaluate and treat whatever it is that brought you to their office that day, check your vitals, and usher you out. A discussion regarding the best anti-aging supplements for you doesn't figure into their schedule. This is the kind of doctor you want to avoid, if at all possible.

Know Your Needs

People who get their health care through a managed care plan may feel they are stuck with whichever doctor they first see, but this usually isn't the case. While there are restrictions, most managed care plans offer a selection of physicians from which to choose. Before you pick up the phone, ask yourself the following:

- How important is the gender of your physician?

- How aggressively do you want your health treated?
- Would you feel more comfortable with an advanced practice nurse, such as a nurse practitioner or physician's assistant, as your primary care provider? Studies have shown that advanced practice nurses are more holistic in their approach to health care and are usually able to spend more time with their patients.

Things to Consider

Communication is the key to success in choosing a physician. When evaluating prospective physicians, consider the following questions:

- Will this doctor take the time to talk and listen to me?
- Will this doctor answer my questions and provide me with sufficient information to make decisions?
- Will this doctor be willing to thoroughly discuss my concerns?
- Is this doctor available by telephone? How about by e-mail?

- Can I have faith and place my trust in him or her?

Other items to consider when choosing a doctor include his ability or willingness to do the following:

- Plan ahead to prevent problems.
- Review your total health program regularly.
- Prescribe medication carefully and only when needed.
- Emphasize preventative care and maintenance of good health. (This means helping you lose weight or stop smoking if you ask him or her to.)

Consider Your Options

If you are a member of a managed care plan, you were probably given a list of doctors in your area and asked to choose one as your primary care physician. But if you are not a member of a managed care program or are new to an area, things can be a little more difficult. The one thing you should NOT do is select your doctor from the

Yellow Pages. Instead, ask friends and relatives for recommendations or call the county or state medical society for a referral list. Avoid commercial hospital or physician referral services because they often have a bias toward members, some of whom may have paid for the privilege of being listed.

Once you have narrowed your list, call to see whether the physician is accepting new patients and, if so, whether you can make an appointment for a brief patient interview. Some doctors will say yes, and some won't. If you do receive an appointment, expect to be charged. Consider it money well spent if it helps you find the perfect doctor for you.

What to Ask

Questions to ask during your interview include the following:

- What are his or her office hours?
- Who is the on-call doctor when his or her office is closed?

- How long does it usually take to get an appointment for a routine visit?
- How much time is allowed for initial and routine visits?
- How are medical emergencies handled?
- Will the doctor discuss medical concerns over the phone?
- Does the doctor make house calls?
- Does the doctor have hospital privileges? Where?
- What are the payment policies?
- What kinds of insurance does he or she accept?

Describe your needs and expectations and ask to what degree you will be allowed to share in your medical decision-making. Ideally, the relationship will be fifty-fifty; avoid a doctor who scorns patient input or seems to have a God complex. It's during your interview or initial visit that you should bring up the issue of anti-aging and how important it is to you. Avoid doctors who scoff at the notion or don't want to be bothered.

Lifetime Checkups

Preventing illness means staying on top of your health through regular exams and checkups. As each stage in life presents new challenges, knowing what to watch for can be paramount to prevention and treatment. Here is a loose schedule of what you should keep an eye on through the various stages of your life.

Twenties and Thirties

You should be tested for HIV and hepatitis if you engage in unprotected sex. Blood pressure should be checked at least every two years, skin every three years, and cholesterol every five years. You should also conduct a skin self-exam every month and receive a tetanus booster at least once every ten years. Women should receive a pelvic exam annually, a Pap test every one to two years, and a clinical breast exam every year, and they should perform a breast self-exam every month. Men should perform a testicular self-exam monthly.

Forties

Blood pressure should be tested at least every two years, cholesterol every five years, and skin every three years. You should also have an eye exam every three years. And you should receive a fasting plasma glucose test every three years after age forty-five. Women should receive a pelvic exam every year, a Pap test every one to two years, a mammogram every one to two years (depending on risk factors), and a clinical breast exam every year, and they should perform a breast self-exam monthly. As women approach menopause, it's also a good idea to get a bone mineral density test. Men should receive an annual digital rectal exam if there is a strong family history of prostate cancer or if they are African-American, and a prostate specific antigen (PSA) test every year if they are at high risk. Men should also perform a testicular self-exam every month.

Fifties and Older

You should receive an eye exam every two to four years (annually after sixty-five), a fasting plasma glucose test every three years, a thyroid-stimulating hormone test every three to five years if sixty or older, a cholesterol test every five years (every three years after sixty), a fecal occult blood test annually, a sigmoidoscopy at fifty, and a colonoscopy every ten years after that. You should also have your blood pressure checked at least once a year, preferably more often. Immunizations should include a pneumonia shot once after age sixty-five and a flu shot annually after sixty-five or if you are in a high-risk group. Women should receive a pelvic exam annually, a Pap test every one to two years, and a clinical breast exam and mammogram annually, and they should perform a breast self-examination every month. Men should receive a digital rectal exam and a PSA test annually and perform a testicular self-exam monthly.

Customizing Your Personal Anti-Aging Plan

Now that you've established that you're going to take a proactive approach toward anti-aging and you've found the physician who's right for you, it's time to plan.

We all have different needs and goals, and these, rather than fads, should determine your individual program.

In an effort to help start you out, take a look at the following general outline designed to help you customize your personal anti-aging plan:

- **Identify your goals.** Obviously, your primary goal will be to add as many active years to your life as possible. What else do you hope to accomplish? A comprehensive but realistic list will help you achieve your goals.
- **Develop a game plan.** You need a workable plan—one you can live with. Be realistic in what you hope to accomplish and how.
- **Do your homework.** Stay informed about what's currently available in anti-aging medicine and technology, as well as what the future will hold. Pay attention to breakthroughs in nutrition, because that's where many researchers believe the key to longevity will be found. Talk with your physician about what you've read and solicit his or her advice on what else you can do to improve and maintain your health.

- **Develop a healthy sense of skepticism.** A lot of products, particularly in the areas of cosmeceuticals and dietary supplements, are touted for their anti-aging effects, but there is no magic bullet.

- **Eliminate bad habits.** If you smoke, quit. If you drink too much, stop or at least drink more moderately. If you aren't getting enough exercise, join a gym. Make a concerted effort to add more fresh items to your daily diet. If you can't remember the last time you saw a doctor, make an appointment for a checkup. Do what you must to make your lifestyle more healthful in every way.

- **Know your genetic history.** Awareness of the conditions or medical problems that have occurred in your family can often help you prevent them or, at the very least, prepare for their possibility. If you're unsure how older family members died, ask those who knew them or check their death certificates. At the very least, you should have this information on members of your immediate family—your parents, grandparents, siblings, aunts, uncles, first cousins, and so forth.

- **Enlist the aid of family and friends.** Slowing the aging process isn't something you have to do by yourself. Tell your family and friends of your plan and enlist their help in making it a reality. Perhaps they will quit smoking or exercise with you. Most importantly, don't let anyone deride or ridicule your anti-aging regimen.

Chapter 2

The Lowdown on Aging

Why do we age? Why does time take such a toll on the human body and mind? Why don't we mature to a certain age, then stop? Scientists have a fairly good understanding of the physiology of aging but there is still much debate within medical circles as to WHY we age. This chapter will take a look at the lowdown on aging.

The Physiology of Aging

The aging process begins the moment we're born and continues until we die. Its effects really start to become evident sometime between our twentieth and thirtieth birthdays and are increasingly obvious every year thereafter.

Around age thirty, various systems begin a gradual decline. The immune system becomes less efficient (putting us at greater risk of disease), and the muscular system begins to lose its tone (especially if we don't exercise regularly). The ratio of muscle to fat starts to decline around age thirty, with deposits of fat peaking around age fifty.

Our metabolism begins to change (we gain weight easier and find it more difficult to lose), and our digestive tract becomes sluggish and more sensitive. A decrease in glucose tolerance increases the risk of developing diabetes (especially if we're overweight), and increased blood pressure puts us at greater risk of heart disease (especially if our diet is high in salt).

The heart experiences important changes as we age. Once we pass our fortieth birthday, the heart may enlarge so it can pump more blood to compensate for clogged and hardening arteries. The covering sheath around the heart may thicken, resulting in a reduction in blood output. This decrease leads to a decline in the supply of oxygen to muscle tissue, resulting in a reduction in aerobic capacity. Even minimal exercise hits us harder and tires us more quickly.

Our lungs gradually lose their elasticity until, by age fifty, breath capacity is 20 percent less than what it was when we were twenty. Skin tone and elasticity begin to break down in our twenties as collagen decreases, though the rate at which our skin ages is determined by a number of factors, including family history, lifestyle, and environment. Thinning of the outer layers causes the skin to begin sagging around age fifty, and both sun damage and clumping pigment cells, known as melanocyte cells, result in so-called liver spots and other unsightly blotches. The skin also becomes dryer, resulting in a greater need for moisturizers, as well as more prone to bruising.

The effects of aging are also seen in the hair. Oil glands in the scalp begin to dry out as we grow older, causing our hair to become brittle and more easily broken. And one of the most common indicators of age—white or graying hair—occurs when the hair cells gradually stop producing pigment.

Who has it "worse" in the aging process?

When it comes to hair, men have it worse than women; nearly half of all men can expect some balding by their fiftieth birthday.

The brain is also affected by age. Researchers note that the brain tends to shrink an average of 6 percent over our lifetime, resulting in a loss of cognitive abilities. Forgetfulness is one of the most common "complaints" of aging, though it's more often due to reduced oxygen or a lack of use than to Alzheimer's disease or other disorders. Indeed, the phrase "use it or lose it" really applies to the brain.

The advancing years take their toll on the senses as well, especially smell and taste, which are very closely linked to our enjoyment of food. Taste buds in the mouth and olfactory receptors in the nose become increasingly less sensitive. Like most other indicators of age, a diminishing sense of taste and smell may also be affected by a nutritional deficiency, such as of zinc, and environment and lifestyle factors—especially smoking.

Vision, too, fares poorly as we age. A loss of elasticity in the eye's lens often results in presbyopia (an age-related inability to focus on objects that are near), and night blindness may become more pronounced due to a loss of photoreceptors in the retina. Older people often find it difficult to differentiate between colors because the cornea thickens and becomes somewhat yellowish in color. Age also makes us more prone to a variety of other vision disorders, including cataracts, glaucoma, diabetic retinopathy, and macular degeneration. Dry-eye is a common complaint among many older people because of diminishing tear production, and there may also be a wrinkling and loosening of the skin around the eyelids due to loss of tone and decreased elasticity of the eyelid muscle. In addition, a loss of orbital fat often causes the eyes to sink deeper into the skull, limiting upward gaze.

Nutrition, environment, occupation, and other factors can also play a role in hearing loss as we age.

A measurable loss in bone density and mineral content is also a sign of aging. Brittle bones due to low calcium levels—a condition known as osteoporosis—tend to afflict women more commonly than men, especially after menopause. In addition to breaking more easily, older bones have greater difficulty mending. The regular consumption of calcium over one's lifetime is the best and easiest way to maintain bone strength during our later years.

Hearing tends to peak at puberty, and gradually declines after that. Generally speaking, a sensitivity to the higher tones is the first to go, particularly among men.

Even our urinary tracts are affected by age. Around age thirty, the kidneys begin to shrink in size and function less efficiently, and the bladder begins to lose its elasticity, requiring more frequent urination. Sometimes urinary incontinence can be corrected through surgery, Kegel exercises, or biofeedback.

Finally, there's sex. In the eyes of many the elderly are a sexless population that no longer desire or pursue regular intimacy. However, numerous studies have found this to be completely untrue; the majority of older people continue to enjoy a healthy and fulfilling sex life well into their seventies, eighties, and beyond.

Still, the passing years do result in some changes. Most women experience menopause around age fifty, when their estrogen level plummets and ovulation comes to an end. The lack of estrogen in the system often results in thinning of the vaginal tissue and reduced lubrication during arousal, all of which can make intercourse painful if precautions, such as the use of a lubricant, are not taken. Some women also experience a loss of libido following menopause.

Men experience numerous age-related changes in sexual function as well. After age forty, the strength of their erections gradually begins to decrease, as does the volume and intensity of their ejaculations. Older men also require more time to "rest up" between sexual encounters and may experience a loss of libido and other problems due to a deficiency of testosterone or other hormones.

The Psychological Effects of Aging

Most researchers now consider psychology just as important as physiology when discussing the process and ways to slow it down. The reason: How you mentally approach the passage of time has a lot to do with how happy and active you will be in your later years.

Many factors come into play in determining our psychological attitude as we age. Take health, for example. People who are in good health will almost certainly enjoy their later years far more than those who are chronically ill.

Financial status can also play an important role in our psychological view of aging. Older people with an expendable income have much more freedom than those who are on a fixed income, and this situation can have a dramatic impact on whether individuals view their senior years as a time of travel, adventure, and knowledge or as a time of poverty, reduced activity, and dwindling social interaction.

Equally important to the psychological component of aging is social support. Social interaction and support—an extremely vital component of successful and happy aging—has, in many cases, become increasingly difficult to find and maintain. Many seniors, especially those who are widowed, spend their days alone, often depressed. It's no way to live the final years of one's life, yet tens of thousands of Americans do it, despite the best efforts of churches and social agencies.

> As might be expected, older individuals who spend their days alone and doing nothing are not eager to face tomorrow, much less the next five or ten or twenty years

Of course, it's easy—and incorrect—to paint too gloomy a picture of aging. For a growing number of people, the senior years are seen as a time of freedom and opportunity. Child rearing is over, they're retired, and they have everything to look forward to. They're psychologically comfortable with a process they can't stop but can, in many ways, help control.

The Emotional Effects of Aging

Old age shouldn't have too much of an emotional impact on people in good physical and mental health. If older individuals are financially secure and have a support base, they can expect to remain happy and content, no matter how old they are.

Unexpected physical and cognitive changes, however, can result in a wide array of negative emotions. This is especially true among people who find themselves afflicted with chronic illness, impaired mobility, and/or dwindling social support. All of this is understandable. No one wants to watch youth slowly give way to an increasingly nonfunctioning body or mind, not to mention the loss of independence that often goes with it.

The physical effects of aging can be devastating, as well as financially and emotionally costly. But the loss of cognitive function from age-related dementia is often more so. Many forms of dementia are slow to develop, giving the afflicted person plenty of time to dwell on his or her bleak future. This often leads to incapacitating depression and a host of other negative emotions that can have serious physical consequences as well. During times such as these, loving support from family, friends, and clergy is vital to helping older people maintain their emotional strength and equilibrium.

The emotional component of aging must be an important part of all anti-aging research. The goal must be not only added years in good physical health but also strong psychological and emotional health as well.

Maintaining Mental Acuity

Keeping the brain nimble isn't a quest just for seniors; it's something we should strive for throughout our lives. By exercising our brain on a regular basis while we're young, we all but guarantee that cognitive function will remain in top form as we age.

Among older people, memory is the most commonly affected cognitive ability. Everyone's mind goes blank now and then. But for many people, these "senior moments" occur with frightening regularity. If this sounds like you, don't panic; your experiences are completely normal and easy to fix with a little effort.

According to researchers, older people are particularly prone to losing what's known as explicit memory—the ability to remember a fact on demand. This often occurs when trying to recall the name of a close friend or a vacation spot you've visited for years. The information is well known and on the tip of your tongue, but you just can't quite get it.

What's interesting is that other types of memory usually don't decline with age. Working memory—the learned routines that get us through the day—remains strong, as does long-term memory. In fact, long-term memory is usually the last to go, as often demonstrated by older individuals afflicted with dementia in the form of Alzheimer's disease.

The most striking area in which older people and younger people differ is in how they remember. In general, younger people are more adept at learning and retaining information in the face of distractions. Their brains, it seems, are better at multitasking. Older people, as a rule, require a quieter environment in which to digest new information.

Studies have concluded that this generational difference in learning and memorizing is due to the fact that older people have greater difficulty filtering out useless stimuli, such as music or conversation. Their brains absorb everything, affecting the memorization of pertinent information.

Other cognitive problems often experienced by older people include difficulty understanding or completing math problems, and difficulty figuring out visual-spatial puzzles. While sometimes a sign of early dementia, these problems most often are simply the result of mental inactivity, of not sufficiently exercising the brain in these particular areas.

Research has proved the success of training when it comes to maintaining our mental abilities. In one study, scientists evaluated the number of words people could recall after listening to a lengthy list of random words. Before they received memory training, the older members of the study group were able to recall fewer words than the younger members. But after just a handful of memory training sessions, which included tips such as placing words in meaningful groups rather then trying to memorize them out of context, the older participants were able to triple their word recall.

What can you do to maintain cognitive function? Plenty. Here are some general tips:

- **Enhance your memorization at every opportunity and take advantage of the challenges life presents every day.** For example, when introduced to someone new, repeat the person's name to yourself three times and use it in conversation. See how well you remember the name the next morning.

- **Another memory trick is to turn a grocery run into a game.** After you've made a written list of your needs, memorize it to the best of your ability by taking a mental walk through your kitchen and pantry. Shop without referring to the list and see how well you've done before checking out. If your memory is sharp, you'll probably be able to remember almost everything.

- **Stimulate your brain by doing puzzles and word games.** Puzzles are a great way to strengthen and maintain several different areas of cognitive function, including memory and visual-spatial areas.

- **Read as much as you can and focus on works that challenge you.** Read carefully, with memory and recall in mind. To help you assimilate this new information, discuss it with friends.

- **Take continuing education classes.** Education is never a bad thing, and studies have shown that the more education you receive, the better your mental acuity—and the longer you will retain it. Take a class that challenges your thought processes.

- **Teach a continuing education class.** In addition to the joy that comes with sharing your life wisdom, teaching helps strengthen mental function through reading, self-learning, and lecturing. Everyone is adept at something, so choose your specialty, approach a local continuing education program, and improve the world with your knowledge. You don't need a teaching degree, just experience.

- **Learn a foreign language.** Being multilingual is beneficial these days, and learning a foreign language can also be mentally challenging because it requires the thoughtful assimilation of new information and a strong memory.

- **Start a hobby that requires coordination between multiple brain regions,** such as dancing, painting, or learning a musical instrument.

- **Improve your mathematical abilities by doing calculations in your head whenever possible.** Reliance on technology tends to dull our math skills, a situation that only worsens with age.

- **Write your autobiography.** This can be a very rewarding activity in that you preserve your life experiences for the benefit of other family members and exercise your brain in the process. Recalling previous events requires a strong memory (which may be aided by going through photo albums, letters, etc.), and the act of writing improves visual-spatial skills.

Chapter 3

Exercise and Nutrition

Do you take nutrition into consideration when planning your meals, or is convenience the most important factor? Do you make an effort to exercise at least four times a week? While many factors that affect aging are uncontrollable, exercise and diet are two areas where the control is in your hands.

The Importance of Exercise

Regular physical activity keeps our muscles toned and strong, helps us maintain our ideal weight by burning calories, maintains bone strength and density, and improves and maintains heart and lung function. Exercise also builds stamina, improves flexibility, boosts our immune system, makes sex more fun, reduces our risk of cancer, improves our reflexes, lowers stress, and benefits our overall health. Further, exercise helps keep our metabolism functioning at maximum capacity, which becomes increasingly important as we age.

Why does the importance of metabolism increase with age?

Our metabolism slows with each passing year, making it increasingly difficult to process fatty acids. This affects almost all of the body's systems.

Exercise can be divided into three specific types: general activity, activities to build stamina, and exercises to increase strength and flexibility. All three should be integrated into your workout regimen.

General exercise includes any activity that requires the use of muscles, such as walking, doing housework, and taking the stairs rather than the elevator. This is the easiest and most basic form of exercise.

Exercises that increase stamina involve more exertion than general physical activity and include such things as running, cycling, swimming, tennis, and racquetball. The goal is to strengthen the heart and lungs by working both at full capacity.

Exercises to increase strength and flexibility include weight lifting, yoga, and similar stretching activities. Maintaining strength, muscle tone, and flexibility is especially important during our middle and senior years, and there are additional benefits as well, such as improving bone density and reducing risk of injury from accidents.

If you want to add more active years to your life, it's important that you incorporate all three aspects of exercise into your lifestyle. Begin by evaluating your daily routine to see where you can incorporate more physical activity.

Many people find that joining a gym gives them the incentive they need to perform weight lifting, aerobic and strength-building exercises, but it's not absolutely necessary.

If you decide to exercise at home, try to do so with a buddy. Studies have shown that people who exercise with someone else are less likely to give up early and more likely to enjoy the activities they perform.

Most importantly, consult your doctor before engaging in any exercise regimen. A physical exam can detect health problems that could worsen with intense physical activity.

Exercise and Longevity

Clinical studies have shown a link between regular exercise and longer life. When it comes to life-extending physical activity, moderation is best. There's no need to train like an Olympian; too much exercise is just as bad as too little. The key is to strengthen and maintain your body's systems, not abuse them, which is what an excessive physical regimen does. If you feel pain, you're working too hard. Your body will tell you what it needs and when you've gone too far.

The Role of Nutrition

Nutrition plays an essential role in our overall health and longevity. The reason for this is simple: The foods we eat affect virtually every system in our bodies. If we eat enough of the right foods, our bodies thrive, and we live well and long.

The role of nutrition can't be overstated. A healthful diet provides our cells with everything they need to function well, reproduce, and repair damage. Healthful foods also give our bodies the right kind of fuel so that we have plenty of energy and a strong immune system.

The right kinds of foods help our bodies get rid of waste and toxins, many of which can increase our risk of illness, including cancer, if not purged regularly. And they help reduce our risk of chronic disorders associated with aging, including osteoporosis and heart disease.

If you want to live a long time and enjoy those extra years, you have to eat well. That means eating in moderation, eating less of those foods that may not be the best for us, and placing a greater emphasis on foods known for their high nutrition. Fortunately, it's a lot easier than it sounds.

Good Foods versus Bad Foods

Not all foods are created equal. Some are good for us, and some are bad. Some can be good or bad, depending on how much we consume and in what form.

The list of good foods is far longer than the list of bad foods and includes fruits and vegetables, legumes, whole grain products, pasta, poultry, and fish. If you make these items the mainstay of your diet, except for the occasional steak or hot fudge sundae, you're well on the way to a long life.

Dietary Guidelines from the American Heart Association

- Dietary fat intake should be less than 30 percent of total calories.
- Saturated fat intake should be less than 10 percent of total calories.
- Polyunsaturated fat should not exceed 10 percent of total calories.
- Cholesterol intake should not exceed 300 milligrams per day.
- Carbohydrate intake should represent 50 percent or more total calories with emphasis on complex carbohydrates.
- Protein intake should constitute the remainder of the calories.
- Sodium intake should be limited to less than 3 grams per day.
- If consumed, alcohol should not exceed 1 ounce a day of hard liquor, 8 ounces of wine, or 24 ounces of beer a day.

Vitamins and Minerals

The foods that make up a healthy diet contain a variety of vitamins and minerals. Some are more involved in slowing the aging process than others, but all play a role in our overall health. The following advice and information should be included in everyone's anti-aging regimen.

Vitamins

Vitamins come in a wide variety and perform a number of jobs. Every vitamin has a task or benefit that is unique in and of itself. Therefore, as you plan your anti-aging diet, it's important that you know what each type of vitamin is and how it can benefit you.

- **Vitamin A:** Also known as retinol, vitamin A is a fat-soluble vitamin that helps regulate cell development, promotes bone development, and boosts immunity. In addition, by helping to form rhodopsin, a substance needed by the eyes to function in partial darkness, vitamin A helps us see at night. Plentiful sources include apricots, broccoli, cantaloupe, carrots, lettuce, liver, and sweet potatoes. The RDA for vitamin A is 5,000 international units for men and 4,000 international units for women. Women who are pregnant or breastfeeding should take an additional 1,000 international units daily.

- **Vitamin B$_2$:** Commonly known as riboflavin, vitamin B$_2$ plays an important role during growth and development. It keeps the mucous membranes healthy; helps protect the nervous system, eyes, and skin; and boosts iron absorption. Good sources for the vitamin include milk, cheese, yogurt, chicken, green leafy vegetables, and bread. The RDA for vitamin B$_2$ is 1.6 milligrams for men aged twenty-three to fifty, 1.4 milligrams for men fifty-one and older, 1.3 milligrams for women up to age twenty-two, and 1.2 milligrams for women twenty-three and older. Pregnant women require an additional 0.3 milligrams daily, and women who are breastfeeding require an extra 0.5 milligrams.

- **Vitamin B$_3$:** Commonly known as niacin, vitamin B$_3$ is instrumental in the health of the skin, nerves, and digestive system. It helps release energy from food, aids in the synthesis of DNA, and lowers blood levels of cholesterol and triglycerides. Dietary sources include lean meats, fish, poultry, peanuts, brewer's yeast, and sunflower seeds. The RDA for vitamin B_3 is 18 milligrams for men age twenty-three to fifty, 16 milligrams for men fifty and older, 14 milligrams for women fifteen to twenty-two, and 13 milligrams for women twenty-three and older. Pregnant women require an extra 2 milligrams of vitamin B_3 during pregnancy and an additional 4 milligrams while breastfeeding.

Vitamin B_6: Also known as pyridoxine and pyridoxal, vitamin B_6 plays an important role in the body's immune system. It also helps the brain work properly, enables the body to resist stress, helps maintain the proper chemical balance in the body's fluids, works to supply the energy used by muscles, and influences cell growth. Sources include avocados, bananas, carrots, fish, lentils, meat, rice, soybeans, and whole grains. The RDA for vitamin B_6 is 2.2 milligrams for men and 2.0 milligrams for women. Pregnant women need an additional 0.6 milligrams each day, and breastfeeding women need an extra 0.5 milligrams daily.

Vitamin B$_{12}$: This water-soluble vitamin is found in meat, fish, and dairy products, but not in fruits or vegetables. As a result, vegetarians may develop a B$_{12}$ deficiency if they don't take a vitamin supplement. Vitamin B$_{12}$ enables the body to process carbohydrates and fats. It also helps the nervous system function properly and assists in growth and cell development, particularly blood cells. Vitamin B$_{12}$ is needed for the creation of the sheath that covers nerve cells and helps the body process DNA. The RDA for vitamin B$_{12}$ is 3 micrograms for both men and women. Pregnant and breastfeeding women need an extra microgram of the vitamin daily.

Vitamin C: Also known as ascorbic acid this is an important antioxidant and protects the body from free radicals, as well as helps repair damaged tissue. Vitamin C is also necessary for the manufacture of collagen, helps with the absorption of iron, assists with the production of hemoglobin and red blood cells, keeps the gums and teeth healthy, and helps with healing. Dietary sources of vitamin C include citrus and other types of fruit, broccoli, brussels sprouts, green peppers, spinach, and tomatoes. The RDA for vitamin C is 60 milligrams for both men and women. Women who are pregnant require an additional 20 milligrams each day, and women who are breastfeeding should get an extra 40 milligrams daily.

Vitamin D: This vitamin comes in two forms: ergocalciferol (which is found in a small number of foods) and cholecalciferol (which the body manufactures when exposed to sunlight). It is required for the growth and development of teeth, bones, and connective tissue in children, as well as bone and tooth maintenance in adults. Sources of vitamin D include fortified milk, herring, salmon, and sardines. The RDA for vitamin D is 600 international units for adults nineteen to twenty-two years and 400 international units for adults twenty-three and older. Women who are pregnant or breastfeeding require an additional 400 international units of vitamin D daily.

Vitamin E: This vitamin is a powerful antioxidant and helps protect cell membranes from free radicals. It also assists in the production of red blood cells, helps prevent blood clots, and is believed to reduce development of certain types of cancer. Sources of vitamin E include almonds, hazelnuts, sunflower seeds, walnuts, wheat germ, and various fruits and vegetables, including apples, blackberries, lettuce, onions, pears, and spinach. The RDA for vitamin E is 30 international units for men and 24 international units for women. Women who are pregnant need an additional 6 international units daily, and women who are breastfeeding require an extra 9 international units each day.

Minerals

Minerals serve a similar purpose as vitamins in maintaining cell, organ, and system function and often work hand in hand with specific vitamins. The following minerals are more important than others to our overall health.

Calcium: This mineral works with phosphorus to maintain our bones and teeth. Calcium also plays a role in the transmission of nerve impulses, promotes blood coagulation, and enables muscles, particularly the heart, to relax and contract. Sources of calcium include dairy products, shrimp, canned fish such as salmon and sardines, green leafy vegetables, soybeans, and yogurt. The RDA for calcium is 800 milligrams for all adults, though many experts believe more is better. Women who are pregnant or breastfeeding need an extra 400 milligrams daily. Post-menopausal women are generally advised to consume 1,500 milligrams of calcium daily.

Iron: This mineral is an important component of hemoglobin, the part of red blood cells that carries oxygen throughout the body. Sources of iron include cheddar cheese, chickpeas, enriched bread, lentils, nuts, prune juice, and wheat germ. The RDA for iron is 10 milligrams for men nineteen and older, 18 milligrams for women eleven to fifty, and 10 milligrams for women fifty-one and older. Women who are pregnant or breastfeeding require an additional 50 milligrams of iron daily, though pregnant women should not take iron supplements during the first trimester of pregnancy unless prescribed by their physician.

Magnesium: This mineral is instrumental in many bodily functions, including the absorption of calcium and the movement of sodium and potassium across cell membranes. Magnesium also helps nerve impulses travel through the body, helps maintain the body's metabolism, and aids muscle function—including that of the heart. Magnesium can be obtained from many types of fish, fruits, green leafy vegetables, dairy products, nuts, and wheat germ. The RDA for magnesium is 350 milligrams for men and 300 milligrams for women. Women who are pregnant or breastfeeding should take an extra 150 milligrams of magnesium daily, preferably from dietary sources. Doctors recommend against taking magnesium supplements during pregnancy.

Phosphorus: Phosphorus is important in maintaining bones and teeth. It also plays a role in all chemical reactions in the body, helps the body metabolize several B vitamins, aids in the healing of fractures, helps the body produce energy, and boosts the growth, maintenance, and repair of all tissue. Sources of phosphorus include red meat and calves liver, poultry, fish, dairy products, peanuts, dried beans, peas, soybeans, and whole grains. The RDA for phosphorus is 800 milligrams for all adults. Women who are pregnant or breast-feeding should get an additional 400 milligrams of phosphorus daily.

Potassium: This is one of the most important minerals in the maintenance of body function. Among other things, potassium keeps the heart beating normally, helps muscles contract, and feeds cells by controlling the transfer of nutrients from surrounding fluids. Potassium also helps the kidneys remove waste products from the body, helps provide oxygen to the brain, and works with calcium to regulate nerve function. The best sources of potassium include avocados, bananas, citrus fruit, milk, nuts, potatoes, spinach, tomatoes, and whole grains. There is no standard RDA for potassium because requirements are affected by the amount of salt you consume in your diet, though most nutrition experts believe 2,000 to 2,500 milligrams to be a good daily minimum. Since most people get sufficient potassium from their diet, supplements are required only if you are taking medications that deplete your potassium reserves.

Selenium: The primary function of selenium is to protect cells from free radicals. Sources of selenium include broccoli, cabbage, celery, chicken, garlic, liver, onions, and whole grains. There is no established RDA for selenium, though men and women can safely consume between 50 and 200 micrograms daily.

Zinc: This element is part of the molecular structure of dozens of important enzymes, is a component of the insulin that regulates our energy supply, and works with red blood cells to transport waste carbon dioxide from body tissue to the lungs, where it is expelled. Zinc is also vital to the production of the RNA and DNA that oversee the division, growth, and repair of the body's cells; helps preserve our sense of taste and smell; and aids in healing. Sources include beef, herring, pork, poultry, milk, soybeans, and whole grains. The RDA for zinc is 15 milligrams. Women who are pregnant should take an additional 5 milligrams of zinc daily, and women who are breastfeeding should take an extra 10 milligrams.

Chapter 4

Herbal Remedies

The use of herbs as both medicine and nutritional supplements has never been more popular. Should herbs play a role in your anti-aging regimen? Only if you use them moderately and intelligently. Herbs have a centuries-old history as medicinal compounds, and studies seem to show that they work. Let's take a look at the use of herbal remedies in your anti-aging regimen.

Herbs and Your Anti-Aging Regimen

Although the use of herbs for medicinal purposes is not a new concept, many people are unaware of how herbs can benefit their health. The whole idea of herbal remedies may open up a completely new approach toward anti-aging.

Your Herbal Medicinal Choices

The word herb, as used in herbal remedies, is also known as "botanical medicine." These terms mean that a plant part is used to make a medicinal preparation. An herb can be the entire plant or any of its parts.

One way to categorize herbs is by looking at what kinds of ailments respond to their use. Another way is to look at how many of our modern-day drugs are based on herbal components. These synthesized substances, now known as drugs, have been separated out from the whole plant by various means.

There are still a vast number of plants that may hold hidden cures for some of humanity's most perplexing diseases, such as cancer, AIDS, diabetes, or other illnesses today considered incurable. This fact alone should make us treat all plant life, and especially herbal plant life, with great respect.

> To date, out of the approximately 500,000 plant species on Earth, only about 5,000 have been studied for their medicinal value.

Testing the Medical Use of Herbs

It's difficult to scientifically test and evaluate the medical use of herbs in the laboratory. These plants are complex, which may be why they have such a dramatic effect on human physiology. All living things, including humans, are composed of families of related organic compounds. Therefore the proteins, enzymes, sugars, vitamins, minerals, and even toxic substances found in plants can, and will, affect the human system by relating to similar substances found in the body.

Frequently, a plant chemical, when applied to the human system, will mimic its own usual reaction inside the plant from which it originated.

A classic example of this reaction is that of antibiotics, which evolved in plants to ward off attacks by specific bacteria and fungi. These substances act the same way in animals. Therefore, it appears that there may be similarly transferable processes between plants and humans.

There are also many subtle similarities between plant and animal biochemistry, beyond the more direct relationship already described. For example, human sex hormones have been discovered in yeast and certain fungi. Several plants contain compounds in themselves that resemble those found naturally in humans, such as the endorphins that inhibit pain.

The World Health Organization (WHO) is making efforts all over the globe to safeguard the kind of medicine, called "folk," or "traditional," on which the bulk of the world's population depends, just as it has for eons. Their continuing fieldwork among indigenous peoples is of great value and is urgently needed. Plant species are disappearing at an alarming rate and can never be replaced. A vast amount of herbal knowledge gained over the centuries is being lost with the disappearance of the forest habitats—especially the rain forests—and the displacement of their inhabitants, whose information about the properties of native and local herbs and plants is often stored in memory, not in written records.

Medicine of the People

Herbalism has always been considered the "medicine of the people." It consists of simple remedies (in medieval times herbs were called "simples") to be used at home to treat minor ailments or wounds. Herbs have also been used as a supplement to prescription drugs given for chronic and acute conditions. Many herbs can be easily prepared as teas, and more complex preparations can be made at home. Most people choose commercially prepared herbal products available at health food stores and some pharmacies. It is important to keep in mind that although most herbs are considered safe, they can be potent and should be treated respectfully.

Although some herbs work quickly, especially for acute conditions, chronic problems may require several weeks, or even months, of treatment before significant results are achieved. With herbal treatments, symptoms may change as time progresses, so it is necessary to review the remedy and its effects periodically at least once a month and to be prepared to alter it in accord with changing conditions. Professional herbalists who monitor their patients often adjust their remedies frequently as the person's general state changes. Self-reliance and self-treatment are admirable, but due caution must always be taken, especially if the person is taking any prescription medicines for a particular condition. Some herbs interact with prescription drugs; therefore, you should always consult your doctor or health care professional before using herbal remedies in conjunction with prescription medicines.

Never exceed the recommended dose of a herbal remedy, and do not continue with home treatment if a condition worsens or becomes chronic. If the true diagnosis is in any way uncertain, a professional should be consulted.

Playing It Safe

Because herbal medicines have been serving people's health and healing needs for thousands upon thousands of years, we tend to think of them as innocuous and safe. And, by and large, herbal remedies are one of the safest ways to treat most bodily dysfunctions, from the everyday minor ones, such as cuts and scrapes, colds and influenza, menstrual difficulties, and childhood ailments, to more serious conditions, such as chronic arthritis and respiratory problems. Nonetheless, it must be stressed that herbs are not merely helpful plants; they can be potent medicines and, as such, are to be treated with the respect a powerful drug or agent deserves.

Today, we tend to think of herbs as "natural" forms of drugs, but they are actually foods that possess medicinal qualities, and they are ingested into the system (or used topically and absorbed through the skin) just as our ordinary foods are. In fact, many common foods that we don't consider to be "herbal" or healing are now being discovered to possess a wide range of beneficial properties. For example, the common blueberry—the stuff of many homemade cobbler and millions of muffins—has been found to be the most potent antioxidant extant. It outdistances by far the former favorite antioxidant substances that have been highly touted. And the substance lycopene, which is thought to reduce the risk of prostate cancer and inhibit the spread of several types of cancer, including breast cancer, lung cancer, endometrial cancer, and stomach cancer, is found in astonishing abundance in one of our most common vegetables—the tomato! Whoever thought spaghetti drenched in tomato sauce would be good for you? Used as foods or flavoring agents (e.g., garlic, parsley, turmeric), herbs combine with our bodies and are able to address both the symptoms and underlying causes of health problems. Herbs offer the body nutrients it does not always receive but definitely needs. Unfortunately, commercially grown food is often grown on depleted soil as well as doused with pesticides. As we've already mentioned, many people do not pay sufficient attention to proper nutrition because they are "too busy" or simply lack the knowledge or interest. So try to keep herbs in mind as you incorporate proper nutrition into your anti-aging regimen.

Precautions You Can Take

When considering safety, it is important to remember that herbs, when used as medicines, are essentially body balancers that help the body's entire ecosystem to heal itself. If you are going to use herbs medicinally, there are three primary rules you should follow:

1. **Do not self-diagnose.** Even minor conditions could be symptoms of a serious problem. If possible, consult someone who is a natural health care specialist.

2. **Work closely with your health care provider.** If you are under the care of a physician who is giving you prescription drugs, discuss any herbal treatments you are considering with him or her.

3. **Educate yourself about herbs and their uses.** Bookstore shelves are crammed with dozens of books on herbs for every purpose; some are regularly updated with new information.

Beware of Possible Side Effects

Generally speaking, herbs provide a rich variety of healing agents and—as most of them are edible plants—they are as safe as foods and have almost no side effects. Of course, one must always consider the individual who is taking the herbs, and for what reasons. Just as some people are allergic to certain foods and have adverse reactions to eating, say, strawberries or eggplant, you must take your own constitution into consideration. If, for example, aspirin upsets your stomach, you would not want to take willow bark, from which aspirin is derived.

The key to avoiding an adverse reaction is moderation, both in formulation and in dosage. Always follow the dosage recommendations on the labels of any herbal products that you buy and, if you make your own preparations, be sure you have proper directions.

Anything mishandled or taken to excess can cause negative side effects, but these are easy enough to avoid with proper attention and care (just as you wash your cutting board after cutting up a raw chicken to avoid contaminating your other foods with bacteria). The use of common sense is as important regarding taking herbs as it is in preparing food, driving your car, working around the house, or any other area of life. Safety is never a guarantee without proper precautions.

However, as a general rule, herbs can be used freely and safely as part of your health regimen, just as you might take a daily multiple vitamin tablet, considering it not as a medicine but as a health benefit for maintenance.

Herbs for Common Ailments

The whole idea of herbal remedies really isn't as "new agey" as you may believe. In fact, herbs can be used to treat any number of ailments, including several common conditions of aging. From something as simple as the common cold, to something as complex as varicose veins, there are several well-known herbal remedies to help you out.

Herbal Remedies for Osteoarthritis and Rheumatism

There are two main types of arthritis: osteo-arthritis (OA), which is characterized by pain and swelling of the joints, generally due to wear and tear, and rheumatoid arthritis (RA), which is characterized by the inflammation of many joints and requires professional treatment. Rheumatism is a general term for any muscle pain; lumbago is lower-back pain. Symptoms often worsen in damp weather. These are the key symptoms:

- Stiffness and joint pain
- Swollen or deformed joints
- Hot or burning sensations in joints (RA)
- Creaking sounds in joints

And here are some herbal remedies to help you out:

- **Angelica** is a warming and stimulating herb effective for "cold" types of osteoarthritis and for rheumatism.

- **Devil's claw** has a potent and anti-inflammatory action that has been compared to cortisone. It's better for osteoarthritis and degenerative conditions than for rheumatoid arthritis.
- **Bogbean** is a cleansing, cooling, and anti-inflammatory herb useful for "hotter" types of arthritis and for muscle pain.
- **White willow** is rich in salicylates, which are anti-inflammatories that cool hot joints; it's especially useful for the pain associated with the acute phases of arthritis and for muscle pain.

Amazing Garlic

Garlic, one of the world's most popular culinary herbs, also has a long history as a medicinal plant. Indeed, scientific studies have verified what herbalists have known for centuries—that garlic both prevents and treats illness in a wide variety of ways.

Among its many attributes, garlic is known to lower cholesterol levels, thin the blood, kill bacteria, boost the immune system, lower blood sugar levels, and reduce the risk of certain types of cancer. There is also evidence that the herb helps relieve asthma, ease ear infections, and facilitate healthy cell function.

So what's the verdict on garlic intake?

Bottom line: Garlic should be consumed often by those who want to maintain their health and age well.

How to Obtain Healing Herbs

There are three ways to obtain healing herbs: gather them in the wild, grow them yourself, or buy them. Since most people will choose to buy ready-made preparations in their health food stores or from mail-order sources rather than either gathering or growing them, there are some pointers to use when buying medicinal herbs:

- **Whenever possible, buy fresh herbs that are organically grown or wild crafted** (grown in their natural habitat). When buying fresh-dried herbs, make sure they are grown locally.

- **If buying bulk herbs, test a sample by rubbing some between your fingers to check the smell.** Even dried herbs when crushed give off strong evidence of their volatile oils, and so potency is easily evident.

- **Buy the best quality herbs available.** Bargain herbs are usually adulterated. More costly products from reputable companies are a better choice because the growing/gathering/preparation/ storage phases of the process are supported by experience and quality control.

- **When choosing packaged herbs, buy from a company that specializes in herbs, not one that is primarily a supplier of vitamins or other supplements.** Herbal companies tend to be devotees of their products and have a high level of integrity in handling and preparation.

- **Make sure that any product you buy is tightly sealed** and has been kept away from excess light and heat. Check the expiration date.

- **Ask your herbal consultant or health care practitioner what brands he or she recommends.**

- **Do not rely on information about herbs from a clerk in a health food store or pharmacy,** especially if it is part of a large chain store. Ask to see the buyer of herbal products or the store manager if you want information. You can also ask whether they have a qualified herbalist on staff or can recommend someone who practices herbalism locally. Such a person would likely be a regular customer.

Chapter 5

Anti-Aging Tactics

There's more to anti-aging than just watching what you eat and exercising enough. For your anti-aging regimen and your overall health, there are other tactics that will help you. This chapter is going to help you to recognize the importance of breaking bad habits and setting up good habits, as well as address the issues of stress, sex, and depression as they relate to aging.

The Effects of Stress on Health and Aging

Stress is an unavoidable part of life. The best we can do is try to minimize the stress in our lives to keep it from affecting our health. Chronic, unrelenting stress damages our health and causes us to age faster.

There are actually two kinds of stress in our lives—good stress and bad stress. Good stress is the excitement/anxiety we feel when our favorite sports team tries to rally during the closing minutes of the game. Our heart races, our palms get sweaty, our breathing becomes a little labored. However, this physical response seldom lasts very long and thus does us little harm.

Bad stress results in the same physical reaction but comes from physical or mental discomfort. Unlike the sources of good stress, bad stress can become long term, hitting us day after day without a break, until we become physically ill and mentally drained.

Stress readies the body's fight-or-flight mechanism, a reaction that aided in our prehistoric ancestors' day-to-day survival. However, modern stress is seldom resolved by either of those reactions; we can't fight it, and we can't run from it.

It's just there, every day, affecting our health and well-being.

Stress results in a number of physical responses. As the fight-or-flight mechanism is triggered, hormone production kicks into overdrive, filling our bloodstream with a wide variety of chemicals.

Our blood pressure skyrockets, proteins are turned into sugars for fast fuel, and we may even experience a brief period of amazing strength, which explains those tales of women lifting cars at the scene of an accident.

If our lives are relatively stress free, then the occasional stressful event will have little lasting impact on our health. Once the stressful issue is resolved, our bodies return to normal and everything is fine. However, for most Americans, stress is an everyday occurrence. Repeated stress can stimulate the production of cell-damaging free radicals, depress the immune system, increase blood pressure, raise blood cholesterol levels, boost anxiety levels, and promote depression. Common health problems caused or made worse by stress include the following:

- Headaches
- Neck and back problems
- Heart irregularities
- Skin disorders such as hives and rashes
- Digestive problems
- Menstrual difficulties
- Insomnia
- Fatigue
- More frequent colds and sore throats
- Mood swings

Stress also affects our behavior and lifestyle, almost always negatively. When under stress, we tend to look for easy solutions, such as alcohol or recreational drugs. People who smoke tend to do so more often when under stress, and it's not uncommon for women to develop eating disorders such as anorexia or bulimia. The trouble is that once we start these behaviors, it's difficult to stop when our stress levels go down.

Stress Reduction Made Easy

While it's impossible to completely eliminate stress from our lives, there are ways to reduce its effects on our minds and bodies. Following are some helpful stress-reduction tips:

Get a checkup. If you've been under a lot of stress, you should find out how it has affected your health and what you need to do to reduce its impact. Your doctor can pinpoint specific stress-related problems and offer advice on how to correct them.

Don't hold in stress-related issues. Talking with family and friends about the stressful issues in your life can go a long way toward making them more manageable. If necessary, consider seeking professional counseling.

Spend quality time with your closest friends.

Fix it or forget it. Do what you can to resolve the stressful situations in your life and stop worrying about those you can't resolve.

Get plenty of exercise. Physical activity stimulates the production of hormones that relieve stress, diminish anxiety, and improve mood.

Get plenty of sleep.

Pursue a hobby. A calming activity such as gardening or painting is a great way to forget your troubles.

Get a pet. Playing with a cat, dog, or hamster can be very calming.

Get away for a while. Sometimes our environment is the biggest stressor in our lives. If it's been a while since you've taken a vacation, get as far away from the source of your troubles as you can and enjoy yourself. Most importantly, don't take your problems with you!

Take good care of your finances and do what you can to minimize debt. Financial problems are one of the leading causes of stress.

Don't assume other people's problems. Charity is good, but you should think first of yourself and your family.

Take up meditation and other stress-reducing techniques. Fifteen minutes of uninterrupted meditation is a wonderful way to melt away the day's worries and stress.

Improve your time management at work and at home so that you're not constantly playing catch-up.

Laugh! It really is the best medicine—for both our minds and our bodies.

Avoid harmful solutions, such as drinking alcohol and taking drugs. Alcohol is a depressant that will make the problems in your life worse and, thus, increase your stress levels.

Reduce your caffeine intake. Caffeine is a stimulant that agitates the body and exacerbates the perception of the stress in our lives.

Learn to assert yourself when necessary. People will walk all over you if allowed to, and that can add a lot of stress to your life.

Beating the Blues

Depression is one of the most common mental illnesses in the world. It afflicts people of all ages and walks of life, and can have a dramatic impact on our overall mental and physical health if not treated.

Almost everyone feels "down in the dumps" once in a while. That's normal and nothing to worry about. But when a feeling of sadness, melancholy, or hopelessness lasts more than two weeks, it becomes a medical issue with far-reaching consequences and should be addressed by a physician.

Most cases of clinical depression are the result of a biochemical imbalance in the brain and a psychological imbalance in thinking and can usually be treated with medication, therapy, or a combination of both.

The most important thing you must understand is that depression is not a personal failing. It is not caused by something you did or did not do, nor is it something you could have prevented. Depression happens, and it happens a lot. By recognizing the most common symptoms, you can determine early on whether you or a loved one has clinical depression and then seek help.

Symptoms include the following:

- A change in eating or sleeping habits
- Inability to concentrate or difficulty in making decisions
- Withdrawal from friends, family, or other social contacts
- Preoccupation with aches and pains; persistent headaches or stomachaches, or chronic pain
- Persistent sadness or hopelessness; frequent crying for no apparent reason
- General irritability or restlessness
- Decreased energy or fatigue
- Feelings of worthlessness, that no one loves you, or that life isn't worth living
- Thoughts of death or suicide, or suicide attempts

If you or someone you care about exhibits three or more of these symptoms, see your doctor immediately for a full evaluation. Depression reacts very well to a large number of medications, and symptoms usually subside relatively quickly once treatment begins.

Sex and Longevity

Sex not only feels good, it's good for you. Regular sexual activity benefits the mind and body in a variety of ways and ultimately can help you live longer.

This isn't just theory; it's clinical fact. A Duke University longitudinal study on aging found a strong correlation between the frequency and enjoyment of sexual intercourse and longevity. And a more recent British study had the same result, noting lower overall rates of mortality among men who have sex far more frequently than the once-a-week national average.

Bottom line: Men and women who have frequent, loving sex tend to live longer than those who don't.

Working with Your Partner

It's easy to fall into a rut in a long-term relationship, doing the same thing over and over until sex becomes more of a chore than a pleasure. When this happens, both partners may find that their libidos start to ebb, and sex often gets put on the back burner. In extreme cases, weeks and even months may pass between romantic interludes.

This negates all of the healthful effects of regular sexual relations. But keeping the passion in a long-term relationship isn't as difficult as you may think. All it takes is the will and desire.

Sex becomes humdrum for a variety of reasons. The most common include the following:

Laziness. Very often couples develop a technique in the bedroom that initially pleases both partners, and they stick with it to the exclusion of anything else. Once a pattern is established, it takes some work to break it, and many couples find it easier to rely on the tried and true than experiment with something different.

Poor communication. Many couples find it difficult to sit down and discuss their sexual wants and needs, particularly if they were raised in an environment in which sex was a taboo subject. Rather than openly and honestly talking about what they like, they hope and pray that their partner will figure it out for themselves. But this almost never happens. In many cases, a failure to communicate can lead to bedroom frustration and hurt feelings, which only exacerbate the initial problem.

Lack of time. This is one of the most common sexual problems facing couples today. We're simply too busy to enjoy leisurely romance, so we do it on the fly. However, rushed sex can be less satisfying than no sex at all. Sex therapists call this "Social Security Sex"— you get a little bit every month, but it's seldom enough to live on.

Children. As all parents will attest, having a child can put a serious crimp on your sex life. Once you bring the baby home, your time is so micromanaged that sex can easily become a distant memory. Unfortunately, this can create a pattern that is difficult to break. New parents must learn early that spending some romantic time with each other is just as important as spending time with their newest addition.

As already noted, communication is vital to a strong and satisfying sex life. Couples must learn to be open with each other in discussing what they want, what they don't want, and—most importantly—what they can do to keep their relationship vibrant and exciting. Sex should be spontaneous, but there's nothing wrong with literally scheduling some time together, especially if both partners work long hours. If you have to, make a date on the calendar for dinner and romance—and keep it. Do this as often as you can.

A second honeymoon is another great way to jumpstart a flagging sexual relationship. This means getting away from the house, kids, and work and doing nothing but getting reacquainted in the bedroom. Order room service, play fun bedroom games, take romantic walks, enjoy an expensive meal. The vacation doesn't have to be lengthy—a long weekend will do—but it should involve nothing but love and passion.

Sex and Aging

It's a common misconception that growing older automatically means an end to sexual activity. According to Masters and Johnson and a host of other sex researchers, pleasurable sex can continue well into our seventies, eighties, and beyond. In fact, theoretically we should be able to enjoy sex throughout our entire lives, as long as we are physically healthy. However, one cliché about sex and aging is true—if you don't use it, you'll lose it.

Sex holds tremendous value as we grow older. It helps maintain a strong, loving bond with our partner, benefits us physically in a variety of ways, and keeps us feeling young and vital. But while we should never stop enjoying sex, we must recognize the impact the physical changes of age can have on sexual activity. For example, postmenopausal women may experience diminished lubrication and a thinning of the vaginal tissue that can make sexual intercourse uncomfortable (a problem easily solved with the use of a commercial sexual lubricant such as KY Jelly or Astroglide). And men sixty and older may find that their erection is not as hard as it used to be, nor their orgasm as intense. Older men are also more prone to episodes of sexual dysfunction (especially if they smoke or take a lot of different medications), require more time to reach complete arousal, and require more time between sexual encounters.

Physical issues aside, one of the greatest enemies of sexual enjoyment in our later years is inactivity. This is true for both men and women. It's easy to buy into the myth that older people simply don't want or need sex, but in so doing, we deny ourselves one of the greatest pleasures we can ever experience. Following are a few tips for older lovers:

- **Take your time.** Enjoy each other's bodies, make pillow talk, and revel in your intimacy. Sex shouldn't be rushed.
- **Don't agonize over the occasional bout of sexual dysfunction.** It's natural and to be expected, especially as we age. However, if it becomes chronic, consult a urologist to find out why it is happening and what can be done about it. Very often sexual dysfunction can be alleviated simply by switching medications.
- **Be aware of your physical limitations.** Some of the sexual positions you enjoyed at age twenty can be difficult and even painful at age sixty. Experiment to find out what works best for both of you.

- **Practice safe sex.** This is especially true if you are not in a long-term, monogamous relationship. Just because you're older doesn't mean you can't contract a sexually transmitted disease. More than 10 percent of AIDS cases in the United States are people fifty-five and older.
- **Embrace your sexuality**; don't hide from it. Humans are sexual creatures, and sex is a natural part of life. Enjoy this special gift.

Chapter 6

Age-Related Diseases

One of the greatest hazards of aging is that it dramatically increases our risk of disease. Most conditions are the result of age-related wear and tear on our body systems, though many conditions are caused or made worse by lifestyle and environment. In this chapter, we are going to examine how we may be predisposed to certain conditions, and what we can do to prevent age-related diseases.

Common Diseases and Conditions of Aging

Stroke

This condition results when blood flow to the brain is restricted due to clots or ruptured blood vessels in the brain. Without a steady blood flow, brain cells die from lack of oxygen.

A severe stroke can result in instant death or debilitating physical problems, including total or partial paralysis, blindness, speech impairment, and cognitive dysfunction. Stroke is definitely an age-related disorder; incidence increases dramatically after age fifty-five. The most common type seen among the elderly is ischemic stroke, which is typically associated with atherosclerosis.

Stroke is the third leading killer in the United States, behind heart disease and cancer, and afflicts an estimated 500,000 Americans annually.

Dementia

Dementia is a common brain disorder among the elderly and is generally defined as an observable, irreversible decline in mental abilities. In years past, the many different forms of dementia were grouped under the umbrella term "senility," but doctors now know that dementia comes in many forms and from a variety of causes.

Dementia is generally viewed as irreversible, though there are some potentially reversible causes, including drug side effects, emotional disorders, metabolic or endocrine disorders, nutritional deficiencies, arteriosclerotic complications, and certain types of brain tumors.

Heart Disease

Despite advances in diagnosis, treatment, and prevention, heart disease remains the nation's number one killer, accounting for nearly 940,000 deaths every year—the majority of them among people fifty and older. The economic cost of heart disease is equally high: more than $108 billion a year for treatment, lost work time, and so forth.

According to the American Heart Association, men have a 42 percent chance of developing heart disease over the course of their lives. But women are also at risk, particularly after menopause, when the risk of cardiovascular disease actually exceeds that of men. An estimated 250,000 women over age sixty die from heart attacks each year—six times that of breast cancer, which tends to garner much more publicity.

Many heart attacks are the result of atherosclerosis, or "clogged arteries." Atherosclerosis results from an accumulation of fatty cholesterol deposits known as plaque. Over time, this buildup greatly reduces blood flow to various parts of the body, forcing the heart to work harder and harder until it finally gives out. Other contributors to heart disease include high blood pressure and diabetes.

Lifestyle factors such as years of smoking, obesity, and a lack of physical activity can also increase your risk of heart disease.

Cancer

Cancer results when previously healthy cells begin to mutate and grow out of control. Left unchecked, cancer cells can develop into tumors that leech vital nutrients from neighboring cells and organs. Cancerous cells can also travel throughout the body via the blood or lymphatic system, affecting other organs in a process known medically as metastasis.

All cells have the potential to become cancerous. The body's immune system is able to handle the occasional "rogue" cell. However, problems result when cancerous growth exceeds the body's ability to keep it in check.

Cancer can be divided into five basic types: carcinoma, sarcoma, myeloma, lymphoma, and leukemia. Cancer is the second biggest killer in the United States, just behind heart disease. It can affect people of any age, but our risk increases dramatically with age. Risk factors are many, but diet apparently plays a significant role in the formation of many types of cancer. In fact, after decades of study, the National Cancer Institute now estimates that 35 percent of cancer deaths are related to certain elements in the foods we eat. At the same time, the right kind of diet also appears quite effective in preventing many types of cancer.

Arthritis

This extremely common disorder is probably more closely associated with old age than any other ailment. It afflicts one in seven Americans to some degree and, as the baby boomer generation ages, will probably become epidemic in coming years, according to the Arthritis Foundation.

There are more than 100 different types of arthritis. The most common form is osteoarthritis, which generally involves a breakdown of cartilage in one or more joints, followed by rheumatoid arthritis, which is characterized by an inflammation of the joint membrane. Less common forms of arthritis include ankylosing spondylitis (an inflammation of ligaments attached to the bone), lupus (a connective tissue disease), and gout (characterized by deposits of uric acid crystals in the joint fluid). The most common symptoms of osteoarthritis are pain, swelling, stiffness, and loss of motion.

There is no known prevention for osteoarthritis, though maintaining an ideal body weight and good muscle tone may reduce trauma to the joints. The pain and inflammation of arthritis is typically treated with topical heating gels and oral analgesics such as acetaminophen, or anti-inflammatories such as ibuprofen. The treatment of arthritis is a multimillion-dollar industry, and new therapies are being developed all the time.

Osteoporosis

This condition is characterized by a loss of bone density and strength and afflicts more than 25 million Americans, more than 80 percent of them female. Because of the toll it takes on the skeletal system, osteoporosis is the primary underlying cause of bone fractures in postmenopausal women and the elderly.

The most common sites for osteoporosis-related fractures are the spinal column, the wrist, and the hip. In severe cases, incapacitating fractures can result from minor falls and the simplest of acts, such as bending over.

Hip fractures in the elderly are now one of the most serious health problems in the United States. In fact, they are associated with more deaths, more disability, and higher medical costs than all other osteoporosis-related fractures combined. The results can be tragic: Up to 20 percent of elderly adults die within a year of fracturing their hips, and fewer than half of the survivors are able to return to full activity.

Age is one of the biggest risk factors for osteoporosis, followed closely by gender. For example, osteoporosis is six to eight times more common in women than men because lower estrogen levels following menopause cause women to lose bone mass more rapidly. Other risk factors include early menopause, ethnic background (Asian and Caucasian women are at greater risk than African-American women), lack of weight-bearing exercise, inadequate calcium consumption over one's lifetime, body weight (thin, small-boned women, particularly athletes, whose menstrual periods have stopped from overexercising), heredity, smoking, and alcohol consumption.

Diabetes

Most people tend to think of diabetes as a relatively benign chronic condition that's easily treated with insulin. However, the facts say otherwise. According to the American Diabetes Association, the disease is the fourth leading cause of death in the United States, claiming 160,000 lives each year. It also carries a huge financial burden; treatment costs and lost work time are estimated at nearly $100 billion annually.

The ten-year Diabetes Control and Complications Trial (DCCT) concluded that a tightly controlled and managed treatment plan can reduce the risk of long-term complications by 50 percent or more.

There are two forms of diabetes: insulin-dependent and non-insulin-dependent. With insulin-dependent, or Type I, diabetes, which is most commonly seen in children and young adults, the pancreas fails to produce enough insulin to properly regulate blood sugar levels. With non-insulin-dependent, or Type II, diabetes, which more commonly afflicts the middle-aged and elderly, the pancreas still produces insulin, but the body requires more than is being produced, or does not respond properly to it. This phenomenon is known medically as insulin resistance.

Without sufficient amounts of insulin, blood sugar levels can climb to dangerous levels. As a result, the body's energy level drops and you feel tired and listless. Fatigue is one of the most common symptoms of diabetes, along with frequent urination, abnormal thirst, and sudden, unexplained weight loss. Related complications include reduced circulation to the lower limbs (often resulting in the amputation of toes and feet), nervous system damage, kidney failure, blindness, and heart disease.

Researchers know more now than ever before about diabetes, but they are still uncertain as to its exact cause. Insulin-dependent diabetes may be the result of an autoimmune reaction in which the body attacks its own tissues as if they were foreign proteins. Non-insulin-dependent diabetes is most likely a genetic flaw, though other factors may also play a role, including poor diet and obesity (more than 80 percent of non-insulin-dependent diabetics are very overweight).

The Role of Genetics and Family History

More than 70 percent of aging can be associated in some way with our lifestyle and environment. As noted earlier, almost everything we do in life impacts on our health in one way or another, and over the years, these factors exert tremendous influence in how well we age and how long we live. Fortunately, much of this is under our control, and a concerted effort to maintain a healthful lifestyle can work wonders in counteracting the adverse effects of various external factors.

The remaining 30 percent of aging is associated with genetics and family history. Our genes define who we are and often predispose us to illness later in life. They also help determine how gracefully we age and how long we live.

Numerous studies have investigated the association between family history and the onset of certain medical conditions, but only a handful have actually looked at longevity trends between parents and their children. The 64-million-dollar question in this handful of studies is, does the fact that Mom and Dad lived to be 100 guarantee that their offspring will be similarly long lived, assuming they don't succumb to disease or injury?

The answer is surprising. The studies found an association between the longevity of parents and children, but it wasn't as strong as many had originally believed. The comprehensive Framingham Study, which has tracked more than 5,000 residents of Framingham, Massachusetts, since 1948, found only a 6 percent correlation between the age of the parents at the time of their deaths and the life span of their children. The study's conclusion: If your parents are long lived then your chances of living to a ripe old age are improved. But in the end, a great many other factors, such as familial risk of cancer or chronic disease, will play an equal or more important role in your longevity.

Let's look a bit closer at familial risk of disease, because it's important when analyzing longevity.

Just because our parents lived to be 100 and didn't develop a genetically predisposed illness doesn't mean we're automatically out of the woods. We must also look at our grandparents, aunts, uncles, cousins, and siblings.

Did all of our relatives live a long time in good health, or did cancer, heart disease, diabetes, or stroke afflict a noticeable percentage? The closer the family relationship, the more important their health and longevity in relation to our own. They, just as much as our parents, are indicators of what possibly lies ahead. The question remains: Is there anything we can do about it?

Prevention of Aging Diseases

The first step toward adding more years to your life and more life to your years—the goal of all anti-aging efforts—is to do what you can to prevent or slow the many diseases that occur with age. Not surprisingly, almost all of these disorders have a lifestyle or environmental component to their development. If you improve your lifestyle and/or your environment, you'll be well on your way to reducing your risk of serious illness.

Heart disease, for example, is often the result of a lifetime of rich, fatty foods, too little exercise, and, typically, years of smoking. If this sounds like you, don't worry; it's never too late to start living more healthfully. The human body is an amazingly resilient machine, and even years of abuse can be corrected with some simple changes in lifestyle. You can reduce your cholesterol level by eating less meat and more fruits, vegetables, grains, and legumes, for instance; doing so will lay the groundwork for keeping your heart healthy and strong for many, many years to come.

The risk of stroke is decreased by controlling high blood pressure. Other risk factors include a diet too high in cholesterol, smoking, and a lack of exercise. If you start eating right, working out more, and avoiding tobacco, you'll be doing both your heart and your brain a favor. They'll repay your efforts with decades more of faithful service.

Many types of cancer, as noted earlier, have a strong nutritional and environmental component. Potentially dangerous foods include those high in fat and low in fiber, grilled or charred meats, and alcohol. (While some studies suggest that moderate alcohol consumption has some beneficial effects, most studies have found a higher rate of cancer among those who drink.) Environmental factors include tobacco use (or breathing secondhand smoke) and exposure to pesticides and other harmful chemicals, which occurs in many occupations.

> To hedge your bet against cancer, pack your diet with known cancer-fighting foods such as broccoli, cauliflower, brussels sprouts, tomatoes and tomato products, carrots, citrus fruit, garlic, and onions.

The addition of high-fiber foods is also a good idea because fiber helps move food through the digestive system. Examples of high-fiber foods include apples, prunes, brown rice, whole wheat bread, beans, and peas. In addition, avoid environmental pollutants whenever possible, and wear protective clothing and face masks when working with pesticides and other dangerous chemicals.

Osteoporosis is best prevented by making sure you consume plenty of bone-strengthening calcium throughout your life. But again, even if you've been negligent, it's never too late to start eating a calcium-rich diet, choosing calcium-fortified foods, and taking calcium supplements. Exercises, especially weight-bearing activities, are also good for maintaining bone strength and density. And finally, don't smoke; it inhibits calcium absorption.

Because of its very nature, osteoarthritis is more difficult to prevent. However, doctors say you can hedge your bet by avoiding bone and joint injuries (trauma is considered a primary risk factor), eating well, and maintaining your ideal weight. And don't worry that exercise will increase your risk of developing arthritis; several clinical studies have concluded that regular physical activity has no bearing on the formation of the disease in older men and women.

Obesity is one of the primary causes of diabetes, so prevention obviously begins with proper diet and weight maintenance. And, again, regular exercise—meaning at least four times a week—can also help keep this potentially deadly disorder at bay. If you find that you have several of the most common symptoms of diabetes, see your doctor immediately for a diagnostic workup. Early detection can make management easier and, in turn, reduce the risk of serious complications.

Chapter 7

Take a Look Around

In this chapter, we'll examine environmental issues facing us today, their influence on our health and longevity, and what you must do to eliminate the most serious hazards. There are some life factors that we can't control, such as accidents at the hands of others, but regular vigilance can still improve our quality of life and our hopes for the future.

Longevity and Your Environment

Our environment has as much impact on our health and longevity as does our diet and lifestyle. It may very well play an even greater role, because very often the conditions of our environment are so subtle that we don't even think about them until it's too late to make changes.

When talking about environment, it's a fairly broad term that encompasses everything from the air quality of your office, to pesticide exposure when working in your garden, to how well you have "accident proofed" your home. All of these and many other factors affect our health every day and can play a role in how well we age and how long we live.

Environment is just one aspect of our longevity plan, but it's a vitally important one, more so than many others because it also affects our loved ones. Radon exposure via a cracked cellar floor, for example, means a greater risk of cancer not only to us but also to everyone who spends time in that basement. Similarly, a failure to correct potential accident risks in every room of the house puts every occupant in jeopardy. So you see, a safe and controlled environment means a longer and safer life for everyone concerned.

Common Environmental Hazards

Today, awareness of the impact our environment can have on us has never been higher. Depending on where we live, we question the quality of the air we breathe, the water we drink, and the food we eat. Is it safe? Could it be safer? And how about our work environment? Is our building "sick"? Are we being exposed to toxic chemicals?

In today's world, it's easy to become paranoid, especially if you regularly read the newspaper or watch the evening news. Every day, it seems, researchers are discovering that something we've long taken for granted as safe is, in fact, harmful to our health.

Just how much trouble are we in, anyway?

That's a difficult question to answer. Certain environmental risks are unquestionable; others are open to serious debate.

This issue is clouded further as researchers learn more about the effects certain chemicals and compounds have on the human body and try to ascertain their risk. It's accurate to say that the majority of Americans are relatively safe from the most serious environmental hazards, though constant monitoring is important because the situation can change in a heartbeat. A municipal water source, for example, can be pure one day and contaminated the next, requiring users to either boil their drinking water or buy bottled water until the problem has been corrected. Fortunately, such situations are usually quickly reported by the local press and corrected without delay. But if you don't know about the problem, your risk of exposure to potential health hazards is high.

It's important not to let your fears get the best of you. Scary news story after scary news story can cause even the most rational persons to question virtually everything in their environment. But as long as you remain knowledgeable and aware, you and your family should have nothing to worry about.

Routes of Exposure

It's important to understand the three basic routes of exposure to environmental agents. They are the skin, gastrointestinal tract, and lungs.

The skin is our first line of defense in protecting the inside of the body from the outside environment. Skin is tough and offers very good protection from most pollutants, but it's not perfect. Harmful agents can enter the bloodstream if the skin's outermost surface is damaged in any way.

It's always a good idea to wear sufficient protection when working with potentially dangerous chemicals, such as cleaning products, pesticides, and solvents.

The gastrointestinal tract protects our internal organs from harmful agents that are ingested. Exposure can occur when soluble compounds are consumed, absorbed, and then taken into the cells.

The lungs are considered the most important—and the most vulnerable—route of exposure to environmental toxins. Potentially dangerous airborne agents can be deposited in the lungs and, if soluble, absorbed into the bloodstream. Our lungs are sturdy organs that work hard without a break throughout our lives, but they are very susceptible to certain agents. Smokers are at particular risk because their lungs have already taken a beating.

Water Pollution

Water is essential for human life; without it, we die within days. Water is known as the "universal solvent" because of its amazing ability to pick up other substances after the briefest of exposures. As a result, pure water—that is, water consisting only of H_2O—does not exist in nature. All water has something else in it.

Water's ability to attract other chemicals is vital to our very survival. We depend on it to transport nutrients to cells and carry away cellular wastes, and some minerals found naturally in water, such as calcium, magnesium, and iron, are important to cellular survival. But when the water we drink picks up pollutants, problems occur.

Water pollution has been a public issue and a public worry for decades. In fact, according to one national survey, 70 percent of Americans are worried about the quality of the water they drink.

Is Your Water Safe?

Color, flavor, and odor are not accurate tests of your water's purity. If you have the slightest suspicion that your water may be contaminated, it should be tested in a laboratory.

If you use a municipal water supply that services more than 500 people, the utilities department is required by federal law to test its water regularly and make the findings of those tests available to the public free of charge. So the first thing you should do if you have any questions regarding your drinking water is contact your local water company and ask for the last complete analysis.

It's important to note that this analysis will tell you the quality of the water when it left the treatment plant—not necessarily as it pours out of your household tap. As a result, your household water may contain higher levels of lead, for example, than the analysis reports because lead has leached into your water through municipal or household pipes on its way from the treatment plant to your faucet. If you don't trust the quality of your water, it might be a good idea to have it tested by a private lab. Such an analysis can be tailored for a wide spectrum of possible pollutants, or just one or two.

People who get their water from a private well are at greater risk of poor water quality than those who are served by a treated municipal water supply. If you fear your water is less than pure, contact your local public health department and ask about groundwater contamination in your area. Environmental experts suggest that well users have their water tested annually for bacteria, radon, and inorganic chemicals. If you live within a mile of a landfill, gas station, military base, or chemical plant, make sure you also have your water tested for organic chemicals. And those living in rural areas should be wary of nitrate, pesticide, and herbicide contamination.

For the most accurate results, have your water tested by an independent, state-certified testing laboratory. If there is no testing laboratory within your area, contact your local health department for recommendations regarding mail-order testing laboratories. Foremost, stay away from companies that sell water-treatment equipment. Many such companies offer free water testing, but it's certain that they won't be objective; the test is just a way of getting you to buy a water treatment kit.

If the analysis shows a high concentration of a particular contaminant, get a second opinion from another laboratory before taking corrective measures. Most laboratory results are accurate, but there is always the possibility of a false reading, and you don't want to waste money on a filtration system or other steps you don't really need.

Air Pollution

Air pollution isn't something that's limited to big cities or industrial regions; it can also afflict small towns and rural communities. Nor is air pollution strictly an "outdoor event." Some of the worst air pollution, from a health and longevity perspective, can be found in our homes and places of work.

It used to be that towns viewed air pollution as the price of growth and success. Smoke-spewing factories meant jobs, and jobs meant prosperity. So what if you had a nagging, hacking cough? At least everyone was working.

Of course, the situation is quite different today. Air pollution is viewed as a major health hazard and something not to be tolerated. The Environmental Protection Agency and other government bodies have come down hard on industries previously known as major polluters in an attempt to cleanse public air and ensure the safety and health of all Americans. Particularly effective was the Clean Air Act of 1970 and its amendments, which forced industries to reduce their use of soft coal and heavy oil and required factories to place special filters on smoke stacks to reduce the amount of airborne pollutants they spilled into the air.

But despite these efforts, air pollution in various forms continues in this and other countries and still poses a variety of health risks to various populations—health risks that can result in premature aging as well as reduced longevity. Indeed, air pollution is still considered one of the world's most important environmental issues, and rightly so.

Air Pollution Sources

Air pollution comes from a wide variety of sources. Interestingly, nature itself is a contributor; volcanoes and forest fires pour a huge amount of ash, particles, and dangerous gases into the atmosphere all over the world. But in the big picture, nature has nothing on man when it comes to polluting the air. It's no exaggeration to say we're our own worst enemy.

The combustion of fossil fuels is the biggest culprit, say environmental researchers. Cars pour a huge amount of pollution into the atmosphere every day, particularly in countries where lead fuel is still in use. Power plants and industrial factories also release a lot of gases and particles, despite federal clean-air efforts. Even if a factory is able to reduce pollution emission by 90 percent, which is good, some pollution still makes it into the air we breathe.

According to ongoing air quality analysis, the worst primary air pollutants are carbon oxides such as the carbon monoxide released by cars, trucks, and buses; sulfur oxides; nitrogen oxides; volatile organic compounds such as hydrocarbons, carbon tetrachloride, and chloro-fluorocarbons; and particulate matter such as ash.

Secondary pollutants are formed when primary pollutants react with various chemicals in the atmosphere. The most troublesome include ozone, photochemical oxidants, and particulates in either solid or gas form, such as sulfuric acid and nitric acid. It's these compounds that scientists refer to when discussing "acid rain," a form of air pollution known to devastate forest areas.

Despite government efforts to reduce air emissions, the amount of dangerous substances released into the atmosphere by homes, cars, factories, and power plants every year is staggering.

According to the Environmental Protection Agency, billions of pounds (yep, that's billions) of the nearly 15,000 airborne chemicals believed to affect human health are released into the air we breathe every year.

Improving Air Quality in Your Home

It's never too late to improve the air quality in your home. After all, that's where you and your family spend the majority of your time. You eat at home, sleep at home, and spend your leisure hours at home. Why not make it as environmentally safe, from an air quality perspective, as you can? In so doing, you'll improve your health and add active years to your life.

Your first step, of course, should be to identify all potential sources of indoor air pollution, then take the necessary steps to eliminate them. Walk from room to room and note all possible problems, such as badly vented heaters, appliances in poor repair, and a lack of early warning systems such as carbon monoxide and radon detectors.

In addition, make sure you review all lifestyle issues that could adversely affect the air quality in your home, such as tobacco use, the frequent use of chemical cleaning agents and solvents, and even chemicals used in hobbies, such as industrial glue or paint. Every time you use such items without taking proper precautions, such as opening windows for ventilation and using a respirator, you pollute the air you breathe and endanger your health. Following are some additional tips to keep the air in your home as clean as possible:

- **Avoid all tobacco use indoors.** If you simply can't quit, at least take your habit outdoors. And make sure family and friends don't smoke indoors either.
- **Make sure your home is well ventilated.** Open all the windows whenever possible and consider exhaust fans or air-to-air heat-exchanging devices that draw fresh air in through one duct and expel it through another. In addition, make sure stoves and heaters all vent outdoors. Keeping your house constantly closed tight not only prevents harmful pollutants from dissipating but also promotes sick building syndrome.
- **Keep all gas appliances in good working order** and have your furnace checked regularly by a qualified professional.
- **Have your home checked at least once for radon,** especially if you have a basement. If levels are high, take the necessary steps to improve ventilation.

- **If your house is somewhat older, bring in a specialist to determine if your insulation is made of asbestos.** If the answer is yes, hire a qualified professional to remove it.
- **Substitute water-based products for hydrocarbon-based cleaners,** which emit dangerous fumes.
- **Use environmentally safe products,** such as cleaners made from natural ingredients rather than caustic chemicals.
- If you do use products that emit fumes, **make sure cans and bottles are tightly closed** before you put them away.
- **Always use paints and other hazardous chemicals in well-ventilated areas**—preferably outdoors.
- **When buying home furnishings, select fabrics that do not have a high pile,** which can collect dust and other pollutants. And air out any items that may emit formaldehyde fumes before bringing them into your home.
- **Try to maintain a humidity level of no more than 50 percent** to prevent water from condensing on building materials.
- **Ventilate attic and crawlspaces.**
- **Clean and dry water-damaged rugs and carpets as quickly as possible** to prevent the growth of mold and bacteria.

Indoor air pollution is a serious issue that requires constant monitoring and maintenance. As noted, pollutants are often invisible and odorless, so we may not even know they are there until it's too late. That's why it's wise to give your home a quick but thorough check at least once a month.

Chapter 8

Social Support Systems

Man is a social creature by nature. While we enjoy our own space, it's important that we live and interact and connect with others—family, close friends, neighbors, acquaintances, co-workers, and even strangers. Studies have shown that losing these social connections can have a detrimental effect on our physical and emotional well-being and, thus, on how rapidly and how well we age.

How Social Support Keeps Us Healthy

The influence of social support on our health has been confirmed by both anecdotal evidence and clinical research. But how does social connectedness actually help us stay healthy? What is it about being with close family and friends that does us good? Let's take a quick look at some of the benefits of a strong support system.

1. **Strong social support encourages healthy living and promotes prompt medical care.** Our friends and family look out for us, just as we look out for them, and often become deeply involved when we get sick.

2. **Friends and family are often impromptu "doctors,"** directly caring for us when we get sick.

3. **Our circle of close family and friends encourages a certain degree of conformity,** often conforming to a relatively healthful lifestyle. If few of our friends smoke or drink, we are less likely to smoke or drink. If the majority of our friends and family engage in a healthful activity we too are likely to pursue that activity.

4. **Friendship and loving support can actually boost our immune system,** making us more resistant to illness. Positive emotions can actually stimulate our body to prevent or fight illness, a phenomenon known as the mind-body connection.

A number of studies have found that strong social support provides long-term health benefits as well as short-term improvement. It seems that ongoing, positive social support can work wonders in helping us live to a ripe old age.

The Role of Family

When it comes to aging, the role of family is varied and deeply important. A close-knit family provides unconditional love and support, which helps members deal with stressful life events. This factor alone makes family a vital component in our anti-aging regimen.

Family support through role modeling and encouragement also plays an important role in maintaining proper health. Examples include mothers pushing their children (and spouse) to eat better, exercise more, and be careful when out of the house; fathers engaging in recreational sports with their sons and daughters; and siblings being watchful of each other at school and at play. By promoting healthful living, our families encourage us to live better and thus extend our potential lifespan.

In addition, family connections help keep us young by providing interaction between young and old. Without even trying, young children have a remarkable capacity for energizing and maintaining the youth of older family members. They make us laugh, they make us think, and they remind us constantly of why it's important that we stay young and vital, even as we age chronologically. Not surprisingly, many older Americans attribute their longevity and youthful vigor to doing volunteer work with children, such as assisting in classrooms and youth centers or participating in mentoring programs.

The healthful benefits of regular interaction between younger and older family members works both ways. Young people help keep aging family members vital through their youthful enthusiasm and lust for life, while older family members aid children and grandchildren by imparting to them the wisdom they have learned through living.

Advice and counsel from someone who understands the various pitfalls of adolescence and young adulthood can go a long way toward ensuring that a boy or girl grows up healthy, motivated, and eager to learn.

Finally, family support plays an especially important role as members grow older. The majority of Americans go to extraordinary lengths to care for their aging family members. They care for them at home when they become ill, and when they can no longer do that, they look for the very best institutional accommodations they can afford, visit their loved ones often, and fret that they can't do more. This kind of loving support can go a long way toward extending the life expectancy of older family members and dramatically reduces the physical and mental deterioration often attributed to social isolation.

The Role of Friends

One of the best things you can do for your health—and to control the aging process—is have good friends. Enduring friendship is one of the most important components of a strong social support network, and without it we set ourselves up for a myriad of problems.

Ever-increasing amounts of data show a direct correlation between strong interpersonal relationships and human health, particularly the role of friendship in maintaining a strong immune system. For example, studies have found that people with a lot of friends have one-quarter to one-half the risk of lonely people of dying prematurely and that women with a strong friendship base are both less likely to develop deadly cancers and far more likely to survive when cancer does occur.

How does friendship keep us healthy?

Well, as noted earlier, it often encourages us to conform to a more healthful lifestyle. Our circle of friends can be a constant reminder of what we need to do right.

Friendship also helps us cope with stress. One of the most important ways is by stimulating a feeling of relaxation. This is extremely beneficial because relaxation reduces stress, which is good for the heart and other systems, and boosts the immune system, which helps ward off illness. The relationship we have with our friends induces a state of calm and contentment. We can also vent to friends in ways that we can't with others. They understand us and want the best for us. They encourage us, support us, and are happy for our successes.

Friendship also gives us peace of mind. It's reassuring to know that we have a strong social network, that our friends are a quick phone call away should we ever need them. Most of us carry a certain number of close friends throughout our entire lives. Faces may come and go, but the depth of our friendships typically remains the same. However, our circle of friends can be devastated by a great many life events. A family move, for example, can immediately separate us from friends we've had for decades. And many seniors suddenly find established friendships torn asunder when they are forced to move into a nursing home or retirement community due to failing health.

However, many times a move into a retirement community can actually have the reverse effect; without even trying, an individual may find himself or herself going from no friends to many within the course of just a few days. Retirement communities, which are much more conducive to an active lifestyle than traditional nursing homes, encourage interaction between residents, and most residents go out of their way to make new arrivals feel welcome. As a result, it's not uncommon for someone whose functional ability was debilitated by loneliness and isolation to suddenly revitalize and find that life is again worth living.

If your circle of friends is somewhat limited and you would like more, there are many things you can do, including the following:

- **Join an organization based on a shared interest.** If you're a veteran, for example, consider joining the VFW. If you love reading, join a book discussion group.
- **Do volunteer work.** In addition to meeting new people and making new friends, you'll find

that volunteering actually improves your health.

- **Make a concerted attempt to meet your neighbors.** In today's somewhat isolationist society, it's not uncommon for families to live next door to each other for years yet never really know each other.

- **Explore your spiritual side.** Most religious centers host socials and other events so that members can get to know each other better.

- If you're athletic, **consider joining a team or group.**

- **Consider joining a support group if something in your life is overwhelming you,** such as the loss of a loved one, an ongoing family crisis such as a parent with Alzheimer's disease, or the diagnosis of a serious illness. Friendship and support can go a long way toward helping us overcome personal adversity. The worst thing you can do is hold it in and try to deal with it alone.

Whenever possible, do what you can to stay in touch with distant friends, especially those you've known for many years. Lifelong friendships are especially important and should never be abandoned if possible. At the very least, call friends in other states once a week just to stay in touch and provide support if needed. Thanks to inexpensive long-distance telephone plans and even less expensive computer e-mail, there's no excuse for letting a friendship go by the wayside.

Charity and Volunteerism: The Importance of Community Involvement

Studies have shown that people who regularly volunteer their time and services to those in need demonstrate better health and greater longevity than those who don't. Helping others improves our mood, reduces the effects of stress, and boosts our immune system.

A growing number of Americans are discovering the pleasures of helping their fellow human beings, with the fastest growing demographic being retirees.

Rather than stay at home, a sizable percentage of America's senior population are working at churches, hospitals, nursing homes, schools, libraries, and charitable organizations. Having spent so much of their lives struggling to support themselves and their families, they now want to do what they can to help others. And they're living longer as a result.

There is tremendous satisfaction in performing charity and volunteer work, and you're never too young or too old to start. What you do, for whom, and for how long is strictly a personal decision, but it should be something close to your heart; if you're just going through the motions, you might as well stay home. Consult family, friends, and your clergy for suggestions. You'll be doing yourself and others a world of good.

Social Support in Old Age

The importance of social support in old age cannot be underestimated. It's during this time of life when support from family, friends, and social agencies is most vital, and the lack of it can cause a serious deterioration in physical and mental health.

According to the MacArthur Foundation Study on Aging, considered one of the most comprehensive studies on aging in America, one of the most important factors in successful aging is how many supportive people we have in our "inner circle" and what kind of support they provide.

The authors of the book reporting the results of the MacArthur Foundation Study on Aging use the word "convoy" to describe the social support network we carry throughout our lives because the term conveys a sense of group protection, much like a convoy of ships during wartime. This is an apt analogy; our social support networks provide protection from loneliness by offering companionship and stability during periods of stress and change. This is particularly important during our latter years, when change becomes increasingly common—and particularly devastating. We lose spouses and other family members, long-time friends and passing acquaintances, jobs, and homes.

The senior years are rife with change and instability, and it's during this period of our lives that our network of friends and loved ones becomes ever so necessary to our very survival. Without the support of loved ones, we would be awash in loneliness and despair, and our health would almost certainly suffer.

Studies show that the more diverse our inner-most circle of social support, the better off we are. It's important that we associate with people who share our mind-set—for example, with those who think young regardless of their age—but diversity of personalities and ages is also essential. As noted, older people, in particular, benefit greatly from being with close friends who are younger than them because their vitality is contagious. We stay young by being young.

Likewise, it's important that our closest circle of friends and loved ones be positive in personality. Associating with Gloomy Gus or Depressed Dave will only bring us down and, in the long run, adversely affect our health. Psychologists call such people "toxic personalities" and suggest that they be avoided because of their potential detrimental effects. If you are surrounded by "toxic" family members, try to counter their negative influence by spending as much time as possible with more positive and helpful individuals.

According to researchers, the more that older people participate in close social relationships, the better their overall physical and mental health, and the higher their level of function. The definition of social relationship is broad and can include everything from daily phone chats with family to regular visits with close friends to attending church every Sunday.

The MacArthur Foundation Study on Aging revealed that the two strongest predictors of well-being among the elderly are frequency of visits with friends and frequency of attendance at organization meetings. And the more meaningful the contribution in a particular activity, the greater the health benefit. For example, people who consider themselves spiritual or religious, attend religious services regularly, and are active within their church or synagogue appear to do better than those who simply say they are religious.

> Problems occur when support members such as friends and family offer too much assistance to older family and friends. Constant assistance, while well intentioned, can affect how people view themselves and their ability to function on a daily basis.

They may ask themselves, Am I so feeble that I really need this much help? Cognitive function, like the body's muscles and other systems, needs to be "exercised" in order to remain strong and vital, doctors note. Too much assistance can quickly reduce that vitality.

It's one thing to occasionally assist an older family member or friend when they genuinely need it, but it's quite another to do virtually everything for them in the mistaken belief that old age equals low functional ability. Unfortunately, older people who are constantly assisted in their daily living may find themselves victims of what is known as "learned helplessness." And once on that road, it's difficult to turn back.

Chapter 9

Specifics for Individual Populations

Anti-aging is not a one-size-fits-all kind of thing because human beings are not one-size-fits-all creatures. There are dramatic physiological differences between the genders, which means that certain anti-aging supplements, technologies, and dietary requirements may be better suited for one sex than the other. This chapter is going to take a look at anti-aging specifics for individual populations.

Recognizing Differences

Ongoing life changes make the prospect of a simple, all-purpose anti-aging pill extremely slim. It might be possible if all human beings were exactly alike and our needs never varied from one life phase to another, but such is not the case. We change as we grow, and this must be an important consideration in all anti-aging research.

It must also be an important consideration when creating an individualized anti-aging regimen. The typical husband and wife in their mid-thirties—let's call them Bill and Sue—may be able to engage in certain anti-aging activities together, such as going to the gym for regular exercise, but the differences in their personal regimens are far greater than the similarities. Sue faces dramatic changes in physiology as she goes from puberty through her childbearing years to menopause; how she handles these changes can have an important effect on her longevity. Her physical and nutritional needs will change; she will be prone to different, more gender-based ailments; and her emotional and psychological well-being will also feel the influence. Bill's body will change, too, but in a different and less dramatic way. As a result, while their ultimate goal is the same—more healthful years to their lives—Bill and Sue will have to pursue decidedly different approaches in achieving that goal.

In this chapter, we will analyze the differences in anti-aging for men, women, the elderly, and those with special needs, with an emphasis on current and future health requirements. This is important because one of the greatest contributing factors to extended longevity in all populations is staying healthy throughout life. Staying healthy means doing the following:

- Eating according to our needs
- Exercising according to our abilities
- Maintaining a healthful lifestyle (i.e., avoiding harmful activities such as smoking)
- Taking advantage of anti-aging breakthroughs where safe and appropriate
- Actively seeking social support

Bottom line: An effective anti-aging regimen should be unique to you and your needs, but it should also grow and evolve as you age. Your approach twenty years from now will almost certainly be much different from your approach today, but it's never too early to start planning. The keys to success are self-awareness and continuing education.

Anti-Aging and Men

Anti-aging research, it seems, has a pro-male bias. The majority of available supplements and technologies seem to favor men (with the exception of cosmeceuticals, which are more actively geared toward women), and quite a bit of anti-aging advertising seems to be focused specifically on the male consumer. It's wrong, of course, to think that the anti-aging phenomenon appeals only to men, but that's the way the industry seems to be heading. No doubt that will change dramatically in coming years as new technologies are developed.

Whether men take advantage of the anti-aging philosophies and products currently available is strictly an individual decision. Some pop pills and down elixirs as if their lives literally depend on it; others do very little when it comes to combating the aging process.

The various approaches to anti-aging, as well as the most current findings on the subject, are discussed at great length in the following chapter. There are, however, certain issues that all men should consider if they want to live to a ripe old age.

Men and Nutrition

In general, men are less concerned about the food they eat than women. To most, if it's flavorful and fills them up, then it's good food. However, the anti-aging benefits of proper nutrition are just as important to men as any other population, and the smart man must realize this if he wants to add a significant number of healthful years to his life. Following are some general tips:

Reduce the amount of red meat in your diet. This will help lower your risk of serious illness later in life, including heart disease, stroke, diabetes, and certain forms of cancer. Consider alternatives such as fish and pasta.

(When you do eat red meat, make sure it's lean and well cooked.)

Add more fresh fruits and vegetables. They contain important anti-aging compounds, including disease-fighting antioxidants. Try to consume at least five servings every day.

Reduce your consumption of fatty foods, processed foods, and snack foods. They contain very little nutrition and are packed with chemicals your body doesn't need.

Consume sugar and salt in moderation. Neither adds much nutritionally, and both can cause a variety of health problems, including obesity and hypertension.

Limit your alcohol consumption. One or two drinks a day can actually benefit your body, but more than that is unhealthy.

Take a vitamin/mineral supplement daily. Most men do not receive the RDA of the most important nutrients from their diet, so supplementation is important.

Men and Exercise

More men are exercising today than ever before, but it's still a tiny percentage of the overall male population. Physical activity is essential to good health and a long life, yet many men spend their days sitting at a desk and are too tired to exercise by the time they finally get home.

If this sounds like you, it's time to make some changes. No one can force you to exercise, but it's almost guaranteed that you will feel better once you do. Exercise builds overall strength, increases stamina, and makes you look better physically. It also benefits your body by stimulating your immune system and keeping the heart and lungs in good working order.

For most men, the biggest obstacle to regular exercise is time, particularly if they work a standard eight-hour workday. If you find yourself in this situation, you have three "exercise windows" each day—morning, lunchtime, and after work. And you may have to try all three before determining which is best for you.

Many men find that exercising before they go to work helps energize them for the day. They arrive at work wide awake, fully pumped, and ready to face whatever challenge confronts them. Best of all, their daily exercise is over early, so they can concentrate on other matters for the rest of the day.

But if you'd rather sleep in an extra hour, perhaps a lunchtime workout is better. An increasing number of companies are realizing the employee benefits of an on-site fitness center, but if your company is still behind the times, don't worry—most cities have at least one fitness center within just a few minutes of almost anywhere. A lunchtime workout saves time and lets you return to the office invigorated. The downside: It's difficult to entertain clients when you're doing bench presses. Time can also be a concern in that it may be difficult to fit in an entire workout within the standard forty-five minutes to an hour typically allotted for lunch.

Given a choice, most men would rather exercise after work. They find that it helps them to relax after a hard day at the office, eliminates stress, and reduces their dinnertime appetite so that they don't eat as much. Unfortunately, most gyms are packed after 5 P.M. because so many people prefer to exercise at this time.

If you exercise at home after work, try to do so before dinner. But most importantly, do not exercise immediately before going to bed. Rather than exhausting you, exercise may actually invigorate you, making sleep difficult.

Men and Lifestyle

It is often believed that men live riskier lives than women. This idea could stem from men working in more danger-prone occupations such as firefighters or police officers, but the fact is that men simply tend to engage in more dangerous lifestyle activities than women do.

Men are by nature aggressive creatures. It's part of their genetic and chemical makeup. In the past, aggression was necessary for survival. But today, rather than fighting saber-toothed tigers, many men engage in other high-adrenaline pursuits such as driving fast, drinking hard, or participating in extreme sports such as rock climbing and skydiving. In the eyes of many, living hard and fast is what defines masculinity; you're not a man unless you put your life on the line in some way on a regular basis.

Unfortunately, this mentality tends to reduce longevity by quite a few years. Hard drinkers risk a variety of medical problems, including liver disease and diabetes. Fast drivers risk serious physical injury or worse should they wreck—even if they're wearing seat belts. Participants of extreme sports wager they have at least one life left every time they engage in their favorite activity.

We're not going to tell you not to do any of these things, because that's not our place.

The lifestyle choices you make are your own, and as such, you must live with the consequences.
All we ask is that you take a moment to evaluate your lifestyle and see what you can do to make it even just a little bit healthier and safer.

Extreme sports, for example, can be an incredible adrenaline rush, which is why most people engage in them. However, you should always take a moment to make sure your safety equipment is in good working order; it takes just one error in judgment to land you in the hospital or the morgue.

The same goes for any other potentially hazardous activity. If you think safety first and avoid unnecessary risks, you'll live a lot longer. This doesn't make you any less macho; it's just basic common sense.

Anti-Aging and Women

When it comes to longevity, women have a decided advantage over men—despite the many physical changes they will undergo over their lifetime. On average, women live about seven and a half years longer than men and hold this advantage in life expectancy throughout the life cycle. The U.S. Census Bureau projects that the decided difference in life expectancy between men and women will continue to grow wider until around 2050, when the rates will begin to level off. At that point, say researchers, women can expect to live eighty-one years on average, and men can expect an average life expectancy of 71.8 years.

The reasons why women tend to live longer than men has been a topic of debate among health experts for years. Some speculate that women are just hardier creatures; others believe the difference is due to the fact that men, on average, are exposed to more environmental hazards than women. Let's take a quick look at some of the most current hypotheses on the issue.

Sex-linked differences. One school of thought suggests that women at all ages have stronger immune resistance and are additionally protected from certain health problems by female hormones such as estrogen.

Exposure to environmental hazards. In general, traditionally male occupations expose men to greater danger as well as more health and environmental hazards such as carcinogens. For example, health officials estimate that nearly 4 million workers—the majority of them men—have been or are currently exposed to asbestos and that approximately one-tenth of male lung cancer deaths are linked to asbestos exposure.

Differences in health habits. Women, in general, tend to take better care of their health and avoid potentially harmful habits such as cigarette smoking and excessive alcohol consumption. This isn't to say, however, that smoking is no longer a health issue among women. Recent studies by the U.S. Department of Health and Human Services have shown that smoking rates are gradually increasing among young women despite health warnings and education efforts.

Personality differences. Far more men than women exhibit traits of the Type A personality—that is, more men than women tend to be hard-driven, competitive, and extremely stressed. Unfortunately, while Type A individuals often make great corporate executives, their personalities also place them at much greater risk of heart disease, stroke, and a wealth of other health problems.

Differences in reaction to illness and disability. When women start to get sick, they tend to seek immediate help. Men, on the other hand, tend to procrastinate until the condition can no longer be tolerated. This difference in reaction places men at greater risk of serious illness and, over the years, can adversely influence longevity.

Despite the natural protection that many women experience due to their gender, there are still many health issues with which they must contend and important steps they must take to ensure that they remain strong and healthy well into their later years.

Nutrition for Women

Women have unique nutritional needs with higher requirements than men of certain essential nutrients. However, many women tend to forget about or ignore their special dietary requirements and, in so doing, place their health in jeopardy and adversely affect their potential longevity. We'll review some of the most important nutrients for women.

Calcium

We touched on this earlier, but it bears repeating: Women need higher amounts of calcium than men because their physiology places them at greater risk of osteoporosis, or brittle bones, later in life. How important is this issue?

Consider: Osteoporosis afflicts an estimated 25 million Americans, more than 80 percent of them women. The reason is simple: Women's bones are usually less dense to start with, and the reduction in estrogen that typically accompanies menopause can cause women to lose bone mass much more quickly.

In addition, many women engage in calcium-inhibiting behaviors such as smoking, lack of weight-bearing exercise, and poor nutrition.

Ideally, women should begin consuming as many calcium-rich foods, such as milk and hard cheese, as early in life as possible. Bones grow more rapidly throughout childhood, adolescence, and young adulthood, so it's a good idea to get into the calcium habit at the onset of puberty and maintain it throughout your life. Women in their thirties should make extra sure they are getting sufficient calcium because bone mass begins to diminish after age thirty-five.

Calcium consumption is particularly important as women approach the age of menopause. Once the change of life hits, estrogen levels drop precipitously, and loss of bone mass begins with a vengeance. Those who have maintained strong, healthy bones throughout their lives will feel the effects far less than those who consumed minimal calcium.

The recommended daily allowance (RDA) of calcium for women over eighteen is 800 milligrams. However, some experts believe that isn't enough and recommend 1,000 milligrams daily for premenopausal women and 1,500 milligrams daily for postmenopausal women (and men over age sixty-five).

A woman's calcium needs also increase when she becomes pregnant, because the growing fetus leaches calcium from its mother. Government health officials recommend women take an additional 400 milligrams of the mineral during pregnancy and breastfeeding to compensate for what they lose. However, pregnant and breastfeeding women should avoid taking megadoses of calcium because it can pass into the breast milk.

Iron

Iron is an essential mineral necessary for the manufacture of hemoglobin, the red part of blood cells that carries oxygen throughout the body. Hemoglobin stores up to 70 percent of the body's iron supply, and additional iron is stored in muscle tissue to help deliver the oxygen needed to make the muscles contract.

Iron is important to both men and women, but women need higher levels of iron than men because they lose blood each month during their menstrual periods. The amount of blood lost typically isn't a lot, just a few spoonfuls for the average women. But if iron levels are already low, a heavy period can eventually lead to anemia, an inability of the blood to carry enough oxygen to the body's cells. Common symptoms of anemia include weakness, fatigue, irritability, headache, and recurring dizziness.

Most women receive sufficient levels of iron in their diet, particularly if they eat a lot of green leafy vegetables, which are a wonderful dietary source. However, women whose fast-paced lifestyle forces them into a steady diet of nutritionally poor fast food may find themselves iron-deficient and headed toward a number of related health problems. The answer is better nutrition through a more varied and natural diet, or a daily iron supplement.

The RDA for iron is 18 milligrams for women up to age fifty and 10 milligrams for women fifty-one and older. (Older women need less iron because they cease to menstruate following menopause.) Women also need an additional 30 to 60 milligrams of iron daily during pregnancy and while breastfeeding, according to doctors. However, pregnant woman should not take iron supplements during their first trimester unless told to do so by their doctors. Megadoses of iron should also be avoided because of the possibility of iron toxicity.

You may notice that your stool turns black or gray after you start taking an iron supplement; this is normal and nothing to worry about. However, see your doctor immediately if you notice blood in your stool. It could mean you're taking too much.

Zinc

As noted earlier, zinc plays an important role in a variety of body functions and is essential for general health. It is required in trace amounts, but many women are deficient nonetheless and should take steps to increase their zinc intake through dietary sources or a regular supplement. This is especially true for pregnant women, because zinc is vital to proper fetal growth and development.

> The RDA for zinc is 15 milligrams for all adults. Women should strive for an additional 5 milligrams daily when pregnant, and an extra 10 milligrams daily while breastfeeding.

Too much zinc in sustained megadoses can result in zinc toxicity. Symptoms include nausea, vomiting, diarrhea, drowsiness, sluggishness, and light-headedness.

Women and Anti-Aging Supplementation

The vast majority of anti-aging technologies and techniques can be safely used by both men and women of all ages. There are, however, one or two that are aimed specifically at men and that should be avoided by women due to the risk of potential side effects.

The most obvious, of course, is testosterone. The so-called "male sex hormone," testosterone is responsible for the sex drive in both men and women, though it plays a far more important role in the overall health of men. A testosterone deficiency in men can accelerate the aging process. In fact, researchers have had great success in reversing many of the common symptoms of aging by dosing older men with testosterone supplements.

Some researchers have also had good success using small amounts of testosterone to ease the symptoms of menopause in hormone-sensitive women undergoing hormone replacement therapy. But, in general, testosterone supplementation poses too many potential side effects to be of much use to women regardless of their age. Potential problems include masculinization (unwanted body hair and a deepening of the voice), oily skin, acne, elevated blood pressure, and an increased risk of heart disease.

One last warning: Certain man-made and herbal dietary supplements should be used with caution, if at all, by women who are pregnant or postmenopausal.

On the flip side, men cannot enjoy the benefits of the female sex hormone estrogen, which is produced naturally up to menopause and available in prescription form following menopause. The health and age-reducing benefits of estrogen are many, including protection from heart disease, stroke, osteoporosis, and other potentially serious health problems.

For example, high doses of retinol-type vitamin A can be harmful if taken during pregnancy. And ginseng has a mild estrogenic effect that can cause vaginal bleeding in postmenopausal women—a situation that can easily be mistaken as a symptom of uterine cancer. To avoid potential problems, make sure your doctor okays all dietary supplements while you are pregnant and is aware of any supplements you may be taking if you are postmenopausal.

Pregnancy and Childbearing: How It Can Affect Your Aging

With the possible exception of menopause, few events in a woman's life affect her physical and mental well-being like pregnancy. How a woman handles the many demands of childbearing can play an important role in both her own long-term health and longevity and that of her unborn baby.

When a woman becomes pregnant, everything she does takes on greater importance, from the foods she eats, to her exercise regimen, to her personal lifestyle. A woman who approaches pregnancy well informed and willing to make the necessary changes her condition requires can expect to give birth to a healthy baby, as well as maintain her own good health. However, women with little social support, who are medically ignorant, or who refuse to give up bad habits, place not only themselves but also their babies at risk. And in so doing, they are probably knocking years off both of their lives.

Anti-Aging and the Senior Population

It's not uncommon for older people to believe that the anti-aging revolution has passed them by. Youth is for the young, they reason, and it's pointless to try to boost longevity when you're already in your sixties, seventies, or older.

How wrong they are! The truth is that there are two distinct perspectives to the anti-aging mind-set. The first is that the battle against aging begins in early youth and involves living a healthful life and taking advantage of anti-aging technologies and techniques where safe and appropriate. The goal is not only to increase our life span but also to ensure that our later years are healthy and vital.

The second perspective is that you're never too old to be young, or, more colloquially, you're only as old as you feel. This is a very healthy attitude toward aging because it focuses on the positive aspects of one's senior years rather than the negatives, which is contrary to what our society tends to do. It also places responsibility for slowing the aging process on the individual and forces him or her to take an active role in anti-aging and overall health maintenance.

Anti-Aging Technologies and the Elderly

Many of the most popular and promising approaches to slowing the aging process, such as human growth hormone, DHEA, and testosterone supplementation, appear to be perfect for those sixty-five years and older. These enhancements replace important hormones and other substances known or believed to diminish over the years and, thus, help slow or reverse the aging processing by revitalizing the mind and body. Many men who have received testosterone or DHEA report renewed vigor, physical strength, stamina, libido, and mental clarity—a sure sign that these compounds will play an important role in the anti-aging revolution.

However, as promising as these practices are, they should be approached with caution. Some still require quite a bit of additional research regarding safety and efficacy before the mainstream scientific community will offer its stamp of approval, and others, while generally acknowledged as effective, come with warnings and caveats. DHEA, for example, can lead to liver damage if taken in high quantities. And because the compound is a precursor for estrogen and testosterone, it's possible that DHEA could encourage the growth of tumors stimulated by these hormones (i.e., tumors of the breast, uterus, or prostate).

Human growth hormone is another promising anti-aging compound that should be viewed cautiously by older people. In one six-month study of healthy men over age sixty, recipients of human growth hormone experienced an increase in muscle mass and skin thickness, a decrease in total body fat, and a slight boost in calcium levels in the lower spine. However, a twelve-month follow-up study found that many of these benefits of youth had started to reverse. And another study found that while there were noticeable increases in muscle tissue and a decrease in fat, there were no significant improvements in muscle strength, endurance, or functional ability, nor were there improvements in mental function. Many test subjects also experienced various side effects that necessitated a reduction in dose.

It's interesting to note that some studies have found that another chemical, known as insulin-like growth factor, appears to be the real cause of many of the benefits associated with human growth hormone. The compounds work closely together, and some scientists speculate that one day, insulin-like growth factor will replace human growth hormone as a better, more effective weapon in the war on aging.

In addition to the possibility of side effects and less than impressive results, many of today's most promising anti-aging compounds and technologies are available by prescription only, are extremely expensive, and only very rarely covered by insurance, which puts them out of the reach of many older Americans.

Adhering Your Lifestyle to Your Age

Because many anti-aging techniques and technologies are experimental and still being studied, they may be inappropriate for a large percentage of America's seniors. But if you're still intrigued and feel you would benefit from something like testosterone or DHEA, talk with your doctor and follow his or her advice.

Of course, the latest scientific advances aren't the only way to slow the progress of Father Time. A growing number of today's over-sixty set are finding that living a healthful lifestyle can be just as effective and a lot less expensive or risky. This means eating with nutrition in mind, exercising as much as you're able, and maintaining strong social support.

Diet

A frightening percentage of older Americans eat so poorly that it affects their health. Many are forced into this cycle by a fixed income or other financial factors; others eat primarily fast food or microwavable processed meals because they live alone and find it more convenient.

We've dealt with the importance of nutrition throughout this book, but the elderly are at particular risk. Following are some simple dietary suggestions for better health and longevity:

Eat more fruits, vegetables, and grains. These foods provide much-needed complex carbohydrates and plenty of fiber, which can keep you "regular," lower your cholesterol level, and help prevent certain types of cancer. Fresh fruits and vegetables are also important sources of vital nutrients, including age-fighting antioxidants. Try to eat five or more servings every day.

Reduce your intake of fat and cholesterol. This will go a long way toward reducing your risk of heart disease, stroke, certain types of cancer, and other medical problems. Doctors recommend following this advice as early in life as possible, but it's never too late to start. If your diet consists of red meat five nights a week, try substituting pasta, dinner-size salads, and fish.

Eat more low-fat protein. The need for protein increases slightly as we age, yet many older people tend to eat less than they did when they were younger. In the minds of many, protein means red meat, but as you get older, it's important that you get your protein with as little fat as possible. How? By increasing your consumption of legumes, nuts, and grains. They can be eaten in a wide variety of ways, and they're far less expensive than meat.

Watch your salt. A common complaint among older people is a reduction in their senses of taste and smell, which in turn results in the need for more salt and other spices in the foods they eat. However, sensitivity to salt increases with age, which means additional risk for people with age-related health problems such as hypertension, heart disease, and kidney disease. People who are in good health have less to worry about from salt, but it's still wise to keep your salt intake to a minimum. If your food tastes bland, try a salt-free seasoning substitute.

Reduce your caffeine and alcohol intake. Sensitivity to both chemicals increases as people age, so we feel their effects much more than when we were younger. Neither caffeine nor alcohol does us much good, so it's wise to cut down— if you can't eliminate them altogether.

Drink more water. Dehydration is a common problem among the elderly, especially those who live alone. The solution is simple: Drink as much water as you can, all day long. At a minimum, you should consume eight glasses of plain water a day, and more if possible. Just keep a sports bottle with you wherever you go and refill it as necessary. And coffee, beer, and soft drinks don't count as water!

Anti-Aging and the Differently Abled

The differently abled are often left out when it comes to anti-aging research, but there's no reason why those with chronic conditions or physical impairments can't take advantage of current technologies and techniques, as long as they are medically appropriate and do not interfere with required therapies or medications.

The truth is that the differently abled really aren't all that different. They may face certain limitations as a result of their health or disability, but as long as they live a relatively healthful lifestyle and are in good general health, they should benefit from today's most popular anti-aging approaches just as well as anyone else.

Before taking over-the-counter anti-aging supplements or engaging in any other dramatic lifestyle or dietary changes, it's a good idea to consult with your physician if you have a chronic health condition or disability that could be affected by such changes.

Certain foods can react adversely with certain medications, and some anti-aging supplements may result in physical changes that could affect medical treatment. Even though the majority of over-the-counter supplements are considered generally safe and effective, it's always wise to get your doctor's okay first.

It's important to note that many simple anti-aging lifestyle changes may also benefit those with chronic conditions or physical disabilities. Regular exercise, for example, can improve overall physical and mental health and can even complement ongoing physical therapy. And there's no downside to improved nutrition. Eating right helps strengthen the mind and body, improves stamina, and boosts the immune system. Regardless of physical limitations, exercise and diet are two of the most powerful weapons we have when it comes to winning the war against aging.

Chapter 10

Stay Informed

It is always important to be as informed as possible, especially when it comes to an aspect of your life such as aging. If you are serious about your anti-aging regimen, you will want to pay close attention to this chapter and work to stay abreast of different approaches toward anti-aging.

The Antioxidant Approach

Antioxidants, as noted earlier, are substances that help prevent the cellular damage done by free radicals. Our body produces some antioxidants naturally, and we consume others in the food we eat. In fact, many fruits and vegetables are veritable antioxidant factories, rich with healthful compounds. Even though the association between free radicals and aging is still under investigation, several studies have confirmed that increasing the body's arsenal of antioxidants can, indeed, help diminish the ravages of age and protect us from age-related diseases such as heart disease and certain forms of cancer.

The first breakthrough in antioxidant research occurred in 1969, when researchers identified an important antioxidant known as superoxide dismutase (SOD), an enzyme that breaks down superoxide—one of the most powerful free radicals in the body. The link between aging and cellular damage caused by free radicals seemed strong, but researchers were unable to confirm it definitively. The question remained: Could life be extended by reducing oxidative damage?

Researchers at the University of Southern California wanted to find out, so they bred fruit flies with a special protein that could increase the activity of SOD and other antioxidants when the flies were exposed to heat. The specially engineered flies were raised side by side with a group of normal, equally aged fruit flies. When the insects were five days old, they were exposed to pulses of heat that were expected to increase free radical activity and stimulate their antioxidant defenses.

The researchers were stunned by the experiment's results. The normal fruit flies died long before their six-week lifespan, but those with more SOD lived almost 50 percent longer.

More recently, researchers at Southern Methodist University in Dallas, Texas, created another batch of fruit flies that were genetically altered to produce higher levels of SOD and another natural antioxidant known as catalase. Those flies also lived substantially longer than their nongenetically altered brethren and appeared to age more slowly. Key improvements included more energy, faster movements, and noticeably less damage from free radicals.

Of course, fruit flies and humans are much more different than they are the same, and similar studies will have to be performed on mammals before researchers can state authoritatively that boosting the body's natural antioxidant production reduces the effects of the aging process. But the concept looks promising, and nutrition experts are already touting a diet rich in antioxidants such as vitamin C and vitamin E as a way of reducing free radical damage, especially among smokers and other high-risk, fast-aging groups.

Another important area of research is determining exactly where free radicals perform the most harm and coming up with ways to stop it. The goal, say medical researchers at Ontario's University of Guelph and elsewhere, is to focus therapies on the most important injured cells rather than attacking free radicals scattershot throughout the entire body. Slowing the aging process is one goal of this research, but scientists also hope that it will allow them to help people with degenerative disorders such as familial amyotrophic lateral sclerosis. Individuals with this disease tend to die younger than normal; they also have heavily damaged motor neurons and mutations in SOD.

The results of these and similar experiments are all very promising, but researchers still don't know exactly why antioxidants help slow the aging process. When that mystery is finally solved, the life-extending potential could be explosive.

The Caloric Restriction Approach

Would you be willing to eliminate all of your favorite foods and reduce your caloric intake almost to starvation levels if it would help you live longer? Most people would probably say no, yet this technique—known scientifically as caloric restriction—has proved extremely successful at slowing the aging process in animals and exhibits similar promise in expanding the lifespan of humans as well.

The downside is that you're thin and almost constantly hungry and cold. For caloric restriction to have any kind of impact on longevity, practitioners must eat up to 50 percent less than they normally would. This means going from an average of 2,100 calories a day to just 1,500 calories, eating several smaller meals rather than three large ones, and consuming primarily fruits and vegetables.

As unappetizing as this sounds, some people are actually living the lifestyle. And many researchers say caloric restriction could hold some very important clues to hyperlongevity.

The benefits of caloric restriction were first noted nearly sixty-five years ago by a Cornell University researcher named Clive M. McKay. He found that keeping rats slightly undernourished actually helped them live longer.

Numerous subsequent studies on laboratory animals proved beyond a doubt the effectiveness of caloric restriction. Animals placed on very restrictive diets exhibit an increase in both their average and maximum life spans, and the fewer calories they consume, the greater the increase. Mice placed on caloric restriction from a very early age live up to fifty-six months, compared to an average lifespan of thirty-nine months for mice who ate a normal calorie-rich diet. Nutritionally restricted animals also demonstrate a stronger immune system and have dramatically less incidence of age-related diseases, including heart disease, cancer, cataracts, and kidney disease. This suggests that in humans, extreme caloric restriction can prevent these ailments as well as the development of debilitating degenerative disorders such as Alzheimer's disease and Parkinson's disease.

Caloric restriction has been tested on a wide variety of species, ranging from insects to primates, with very similar results. The greatest benefits, however, were seen in those subjects that started the regimen from an early age and supplemented their restrictive diet with plenty of vitamins and minerals.

It is important to understand that there's a huge difference between undernourished and malnourished.

But as with all promising anti-aging concepts, caloric restriction raises far more questions than it answers. Researchers know that undernourished animals live longer, but they don't know why. What is it about consuming fewer calories that extends longevity so dramatically? And while it has shown tremendous potential on laboratory animals, will it have a similar effect on human beings?

We're used to eating anything we want any time we want, and even greater longevity isn't prize enough for us to give that up. As a result, researchers are struggling to understand how caloric restriction works with the goal of developing a more acceptable alternative that provides the same beneficial effects.

Medical researchers agree that the restrictive diet needed to extend longevity is far too harsh for most people to pursue.

While much about caloric restriction still remains a mystery, most researchers agree that the body's response to the diet is an evolutionary adaptation to periods of food scarcity. In short, when calories become less plentiful, the body goes into self-preservation mode, boosting internal defense mechanisms that increase lifespan. In the wild, the body returns to its normal state once food again becomes plentiful. But with an intentionally restrictive diet, the body is always in self-preservation mode.

Keep in mind that almost all research into caloric restriction has been conducted on laboratory animals. There are a number of people who have aggressively adapted the lifestyle in the hope of increasing their longevity, but it's far too soon to say for sure whether the diet works as well in people as it does in mice. That's something only time will tell.

The Natural Hormone Approach

Quite a bit of current anti-aging research centers around the rejuvenating effects of naturally occurring hormones, raising the question of whether aging is a result of diminishing levels of hormones or hormone deficiencies are a result of aging. Most steroid hormones are available only by prescription and for very specific uses, but word is spreading among anti-aging activists who see the tremendous potential these hormones have in helping to slow the aging process.

Human Growth Hormone

One of the most promising compounds is human growth hormone (GH). This substance is released by the pituitary gland until around age thirty and is very important in our physical development. Levels of GH are highest when we're fetuses, decline during childhood, then increase again during adolescence. After age thirty, the production of GH slows considerably, and in many older people, it actually appears to cease completely.

The potential importance of GH in extending longevity is quite apparent, since it is clear that as levels of the hormone decline, so does body function. Clinical studies have shown a correlation between low levels of GH and a decline in muscle mass, an increase in body fat, reduced immune response, and other age-related conditions. So, the question is: Could GH supplements help reduce these effects and, in effect, slow the aging process? A growing number of anti-aging specialists believe so.

In one of the most telling experiments, Dr. Daniel Rudman of the Medical College of Wisconsin and the Milwaukee VA Medical Center gathered twenty-one healthy men between the ages of sixty-one and eighty-one, all of whom had extremely low levels of growth hormone. Twelve of the men received injections of GH over a period of six months, and the remaining nine did not. The results? The men who received the GH supplements had a 14 percent reduction in body fat and a 9 percent increase in muscle mass.

The men also said that the injections made them feel better than they had in years. However, the effects quickly wore off when the injections were stopped.

Subsequent studies confirmed the beneficial effects of human growth hormone. In addition to a reduction in body fat and an increase in muscle mass, many older people who have received GH injections also showed improved heart function, improved immune function, healthier cholesterol levels, more energy, improved sexual function, and other benefits.

Despite numerous studies proving the beneficial effects of GH on the aging process, the hormone is severely restricted in the United States; as of this writing, the only FDA-approved use is for children with documented deficiencies.

However, GH is widely available in other countries, and a growing number of anti-aging clinics are prescribing it to patients specifically to slow the effects of aging.

Caution on the part of the U.S. Food and Drug Administration is probably a good thing. Despite the good it does, studies show that growth hormone can result in serious side effects, including cancer, arthritis, diabetes, high blood pressure, and carpal tunnel syndrome. Right now, the National Institutes of Health is funding several studies on GH to determine who, if anyone, would benefit from its use and what the optimum dose should be. As a result, it will be several years—if at all— before growth hormone becomes available to the general public in the United States.

Dehydroepiandrosterone (DHEA)

This steroid hormone, produced by the adrenal glands, is plentiful when we're young, though levels drop noticeably as we age. In fact, by age fifty, we produce less than a third of the amount of DHEA we produced when we were younger, and by age sixty, body levels of the hormone are almost undetectable.

DHEA is a very important hormone. It is used by the body to produce testosterone and estrogen. It also helps our immune systems stay strong and healthy.

Like human growth hormone, low levels of DHEA appear to promote the development of many health problems commonly associated with aging, including cancer and heart disease. In one clinical study of men between the ages of fifty and seventy-nine, researchers found that those with extremely low levels of DHEA had the highest rates of heart disease.

The health and longevity potential of DHEA is tremendous, say proponents. Several studies suggest that placing healthy individuals on a regimen of DHEA supplementation can reduce body fat, cut cholesterol levels, increase muscle mass, boost the immune system, and even ease depression. In women, DHEA has been shown to improve age-related osteoporosis by increasing formation of bone and increasing levels of estrogen and testosterone.

Animal studies have been equally impressive. In one remarkable experiment, DHEA supplements helped inhibit the growth of artificially planted tumors in elderly mice, and other studies suggest that the hormone can improve memory and even aid in weight reduction.

However, the hormone isn't for everyone, and there is the potential for serious side effects, researchers warn. Men with prostate cancer, pregnant women, or women with breast cancer or ovarian cancer should not take DHEA because the resulting hormone stimulation could actually magnify the effects of these conditions. Less serious side effects include liver irritation, hypertension, acne in men, and light facial hair in women, though these effects usually disappear when DHEA is stopped.

As the evidence builds, a growing number of physicians are placing their older patients on DHEA to reduce risk of disease, increase strength and vigor, and improve their chances of a long and healthy life.

It's important to note that while the data regarding DHEA's efficacy in helping to slow the aging process continues to build, there have been no long-term human studies regarding its benefits.

Testosterone

Testosterone is often referred to as the male sex hormone. However, women also manufacture testosterone, albeit in much smaller levels—

generally one-tenth the amount men do. Without it, neither gender would have much of a sex drive.

Testosterone is responsible for a large number of functions in men. In addition to promoting sexual desire and stimulating sperm production, it aids the growth of certain organs; promotes muscle, skin, and bone growth; nourishes the urinary and reproductive tissue; and stimulates prostate growth.

The effects of testosterone are most evident during puberty, during which time it plays an important role in the development of secondary sexual characteristics, including a deeper voice, body hair, increased muscle mass, and increased oil-gland secretions (a common cause of the teenage bane known as acne). Testosterone levels diminish gradually as men age, though production can be affected over time by a wide array of things, including illness, obesity, tobacco and alcohol use, lack of exercise, poor diet, and certain medications.

The body's levels of testosterone begin to diminish after puberty, with noticeable effects on physical health. However, several studies have found that testosterone supplementation later in life can help slow or reverse many of the problems associated with age-related testosterone deficiency, suggesting that the hormone could play an important role as a youth-preserving agent.

Several international studies, most of them involving men with noticeably low levels of testosterone due to old age or conditions such as hypogonadism, have demonstrated the hormone's amazing rejuvenating capabilities. In one eight-week study of twenty-nine subjects, almost all reported improved erectile function, libido, and mood, as well as increased energy. Another study involving men over fifty found that those who received testosterone supplements reported renewed strength, increased sex drive, and lower LDL cholesterol levels. And in a double-blind, placebo-controlled crossover study, thirteen healthy elderly men with documented low testosterone levels were given 100 milligrams of testosterone weekly for three months. Twelve members of the group reported significant behavior improvements, including feelings of well-being and increased libido.

In addition to improvements in mood and libido, several studies have found that testosterone supplements can help reduce the risk of heart disease and strengthen aging bones. This is an important finding because men with low testosterone levels are up to six times as likely to break their hip in a fall than men with normal hormone levels.

Prescription testosterone supplements via injection or transdermal patch can be a godsend to a lot of elderly men, but cautions and side effects must be considered. The biggest danger, say doctors, is the risk of worsening hormone-sensitive cancers such as prostate cancer. Testosterone can also influence HDL cholesterol levels and the risk of coronary heart disease.

Finally, the hormone should not be given to men who naturally maintain normal testosterone levels because of the risk of dangerous side effects and the possibility that oversupplementation can inhibit the body's normal testosterone production. To ensure that your body produces adequate levels of testosterone on its own, get plenty of exercise and consume a healthy diet. You'll be happy that you did in years to come.

Melatonin

Of all the hormones produced by your body, melatonin shows some of the greatest promise as an anti-aging wonder agent. First discovered in 1958, this compound—produced by the pineal gland—has demonstrated remarkable properties in everything from lifespan extension, to easing insomnia, to slowing cancer growth. And that's just the beginning, say researchers.

The pineal gland, which is located deep within the brain behind the eyes, is, in many ways, the body's clock. Stimulated by sunlight, it governs our circadian rhythms—the various processes that occur over a twenty-four-hour period, such as the sleep cycle. It also governs more long-term cycles such as a woman's monthly menstrual period. In addition, it is associated with various seasonal rhythms such as adapting to the shorter days of the fall and winter. Over our lifetime, the pineal gland orchestrates the release of key substances, including growth hormones, sexual hormones, and disease-fighting antibodies.

Some researchers believe that melatonin is the pineal gland's "messenger," that fluctuations in melatonin levels tell other body systems when to go to work, how hard to work, and when to slow down. Its responsibilities range from the onset of puberty to telling us when to go to sleep and when to wake up. Without melatonin, our lives would be a mess.

The role of the pineal gland and melatonin in the aging process—and as a way of slowing down that process—is becoming increasingly clear as medical researchers gain greater understanding of the body's internal clock. Once we grow too old to reproduce (around the ages of forty-five to fifty for most women), the pineal gland begins to reduce production of melatonin, which in turn signals almost all other systems that it's time to "retire." Thus begins the aging process as we know it. Interestingly, women have a larger pineal gland than men, which could explain why women typically age more slowly and live longer.

Once we understand how the pineal gland and its vital messenger, melatonin, affect the body and help trigger the aging process, the potential role of the hormone in slowing that process becomes clearer. If we can maintain the level of melatonin we had at age thirty through-out our lives, will aging occur more slowly? In theory, the answer is yes. By tricking the pineal gland with melatonin supplements, we should remain biologically young while growing chronologically older.

Clinical studies on mice show great promise in this area. Dr. Walter Pierpaoli, an immunologist at the Biancalana-Masera Foundation for the Aged in Ancona, Italy, and Dr. Vladmir Lesnikov of the Institute of Experimental Medicine in St. Petersburg, Russia, cross-transplanted the pineal glands between the brains of old and young mice. The results? Young mice that received the pineal glands from older mice began to age much faster, while the older mice that received pineal glands from younger mice actually regained many characteristics of youth and stayed healthy throughout their lifespan.

The addition of melatonin also appears to stimulate the immune system, which usually weakens with age. Part of the reason for this weakening is the degeneration of the thymus, a tiny gland that plays a huge role in our ability to combat disease due to large concentrations of disease-fighting white blood cells known as T lymphocytes. The thymus more than doubles in size during puberty but degenerates by more than 90 percent by age sixty-five. The result is a diminished immune system.

Dr. Pierpaoli studied the influence of melatonin on reduced immune function by adding the hormone to the drinking water of elderly mice. The results were impressive. Almost all of the mice who received the hormone experienced a noticeable boost in their immune function. In addition, the weight of their thymus glands increased, and their thymus cells became much more active.

Studies have shown that melatonin has many other benefits as well. They include the following:

Slowing tumor growth. Researchers at Tulane University School of Medicine report studies that suggest that melatonin can effectively inhibit the growth of human breast cancer cells. And in Milan, Italy, cancer specialists have started adding melatonin to chemotherapy and immunotherapy as a way of reducing the side effects of these cancer treatments. Extra benefits include additional tumor regression and greater patient longevity.

Improving quality of sleep. Numerous studies have proved melatonin a safe and effective treatment for people with sleep difficulties. Best of all, there are no apparent side effects.

Easing jet lag. Several studies involving overseas travelers have found that melatonin can help reset the body's natural clock, easing the effects of jet lag and inducing restful sleep.

Reducing risk of heart disease. Melatonin has shown great efficacy in reducing blood cholesterol in patients with dangerously high levels.

Melatonin, which is available over the counter, appears safe when used in moderate doses (1 to 3 milligrams is common) and as recommended. However, researchers are quick to warn that there are no conclusive studies documenting the effects of long-term use. Erring on the side of caution, most doctors recommend that people under age forty-five (who naturally manufacture sufficient amounts of the hormone) refrain from using melatonin except for short-term use in the treatment of jet lag or insomnia. Those who should never use melatonin include pregnant or nursing women, women trying to become pregnant, people on prescription steroid medications, and individuals with autoimmune diseases such as multiple sclerosis and immune system cancers such as leukemia.

For best results, melatonin should be taken shortly before bedtime. Because of the risk of drowsiness, it's unwise to drive a car or operate heavy machinery after taking melatonin supplements.

The Mineral Approach

The importance of vitamins and minerals is drilled into our minds from a very early age, and millions of people now take a multivitamin tablet every day as part of their overall health regimen. These essential nutrients are instrumental in preventing disease and ensuring a strong mind and body—and some trace minerals, say medical researchers, may also help keep us young.

Chromium

One of the most promising of these compounds is chromium, a mineral that helps the body metabolize fat, convert blood sugar into energy, and make insulin work more efficiently. Chromium is derived primarily from our diet. Rich sources of this important nutrient include whole-grain foods, eggs, broccoli, orange juice, grape juice, seafood, dairy products, and many different types of meat. It is also available in supplement form, which is good for those who may be somewhat deficient due to poor dietary habits.

In addition to the benefits already noted, several recent studies have also shown that chromium plays the following important roles:

It protects the heart by lowering serum cholesterol levels and triglycerides. In a study published in The Western Journal of Medicine, twenty-eight subjects with elevated cholesterol levels were given either 200 micrograms of chromium picolinate or a harmless placebo. By six weeks, those receiving the chromium picolinate saw a 7 percent decrease in total cholesterol, which reduced their risk of heart disease by 14 percent. Levels of low-density lipoprotein, the so-called "bad" cholesterol, dropped by more than 10 percent.

It prevents or aids in the management of diabetes by assisting in the production and metabolism of insulin. To prove the effectiveness of chromium in controlling glucose (blood sugar), researchers with the U.S. Department of Agriculture divided rats into two groups—those on a chromium-rich diet and those on a chromium-deficient diet. Each group was fed a sugar solution to stimulate insulin. The rats fed the chromium-deficient diet secreted up to 50 percent less insulin during the study than did the rats on the chromium-rich diet. While rats and humans are considerably different, this study does suggest that chromium enhances the production of insulin as it is needed.

It tones out-of-shape muscles by increasing muscle mass. Many health food shops sell chromium supplements as a muscle builder, but there's a catch—you have to exercise for the supplements to be effective. That's bad news for couch potatoes looking for a quick and easy fix.

It boosts longevity. All of the benefits just mentioned combine to add years to your life. In studies on laboratory rats, those fed a diet rich in chromium picolinate lived one third longer than those that didn't receive the trace mineral. Researchers are unsure if chromium will help extend the human life span by a similar amount, but preliminary research is very promising.

There are no known dangers or side effects associated with chromium, and the FDA has not set a recommended daily allowance for the mineral. However, nutrition experts advise that you try to get as much chromium as you can from dietary sources because they tend to be more easily absorbed by the body.

Magnesium

Magnesium is an important mineral that shows great promise as an anti-aging facilitator. It plays a wide variety of roles within the body but is best known for promoting the absorption and use of other minerals, including calcium. Magnesium also helps move sodium and potassium across the cell membranes, aids in the metabolism of proteins, and activates a variety of important enzymes. What does this mean to you? It means strong bones and teeth, a healthy nervous system, a balanced metabolism, and well-functioning muscles—including the heart.

The importance of magnesium in maintaining youth can be seen in animals with magnesium deficiencies. In short, they age much faster than normal, are at higher risk of diabetes and heart attack, and show the classic signs of aging much earlier, including atherosclerosis, heartbeat irregularities, hypertension, and osteoporosis.

These problems have also been seen in people with low levels of magnesium. A Harvard University study found that people with a magnesium deficiency were more apt to have high blood pressure, a finding confirmed by a Swedish study that found that giving hypertension patients 360 milligrams of magnesium daily resulted in a dramatic—and potentially life-saving—reduction in blood pressure. And as far back as the 1950s, animal studies proved that high doses of magnesium can effectively reverse atherosclerotic plaques and improve blood flow to the heart. There is also strong evidence that magnesium can facilitate glucose metabolism, lowering the risk of developing diabetes and making the condition easier to manage among those who already have it.

Are you getting adequate levels of magnesium? Probably not. Nutrition experts believe only one in four Americans is consuming sufficient levels of this vital mineral, and deficiencies are even higher among the elderly, who need it the most.

The recommended daily allowance for magnesium is 350 milligrams for men eighteen and older and 300 milligrams for women eleven and older. However, many anti-aging experts believe even those levels are too low.

Natural sources of magnesium include fish and seafood, fruits and fruit juice, green leafy vegetables, dairy products, nuts, and wheat germ. Magnesium is also available in supplement form.

When magnesium levels are low, cell membranes become less flexible and don't absorb calcium as well as they should. As a result, the integrity of the entire cell is placed in jeopardy. Magnesium also protects the mitochondria in the cells, which are necessary for energy production. When mitochondria are damaged in great numbers, researchers theorize, aging is accelerated. Consistently low magnesium levels make the problem worse by stimulating the production of inflammatory substances known as cytokines. These, in turn, create more free radicals and lead to even greater cell damage.

Magnesium is generally considered safe, though diarrhea may result when the mineral is consumed in high doses (700 milligrams daily over an extended period). In addition, people with a history of kidney disease or heart disease should consult their physician before taking magnesium supplements.

Selenium

Selenium was a little-considered mineral until the 1950s, when researchers first discovered its very important role in human health. Since then, numerous studies have placed it in the forefront of anti-aging research because of its suspected ability to prevent a variety of life-threatening conditions, including cancer and heart disease.

Selenium is important because it's an anti-oxidant, working with glutathione peroxidase to keep potentially damaging free radicals under control. It also plays a role in the metabolism of prostaglandins, important hormone-like compounds that affect several essential body functions. Natural sources of selenium include broccoli, cabbage, celery, cucumbers, garlic, onions, kidney, liver, chicken, whole-grain foods, seafood, and milk. It is also available in supplement form.

Selenium levels tend to drop precipitously as we age, which is why it's important that we maintain sufficient levels in our later years. In doing so, we can stay healthy and help ward off the effects of aging by preventing the formation of certain forms of cancer, reducing the risk of heart disease, and boosting immune function. Let's look at these benefits individually.

It's as a cancer-fighter that selenium really shines. Many studies have found that the cancer rate is related to the amount of selenium we consume, with those who consume the lowest being most at risk. In Japan, for example, where people traditionally consume about 500 micrograms of selenium a day, the cancer rate is nearly five times lower than in countries where daily selenium intake is less. Cancer specialists have also found that the blood levels of selenium are lower in cancer patients than in healthy individuals.

Animal studies back up the importance of selenium in preventing cancer. In one telling experiment involving mice that were likely to get a specific form of cancer, only 10 percent of the rodents receiving selenium actually developed tumors, compared to 82 percent of the control group that did not receive the mineral.

Equally important is selenium's role in reducing heart disease and stroke, most likely by preventing blood platelets from sticking together and forming deadly clots. It also benefits the heart as an antioxidant, preventing the oxidation of LDL cholesterol.

Researchers have long suspected that selenium is instrumental to heart health, and a recent large-scale study in Finland finally confirmed it. Researchers there found that subjects with the lowest levels of the mineral were three times more likely to die from heart disease than subjects with the highest levels. A separate study found that the lower a person's selenium level, the higher his or her potential degree of arterial blockage.

As an immunity booster, selenium can't be beat. Studies have shown that the mineral plays a vital role in keeping our immune system working as well at age sixty as at age twenty, and that a deficiency can cause serious problems.

Of particular note is selenium's role as an antiviral agent. In one University of North Carolina study, researchers injected mice with a virus that usually is quite harmless. Then they artificially lowered the test animals' selenium levels. The result? The normally harmless virus suddenly became quite dangerous, breaking out of cells and attacking the muscles of the heart. This effect was not seen in a control group of infected mice who maintained healthy selenium levels.

Because of this remarkable antiviral action, some researchers speculate that selenium supplements may one day become part of the arsenal against AIDS and other life-threatening viral diseases. This makes sense because the HIV virus that causes AIDS is known to deplete the body's stores of selenium as part of its action.

Selenium, unlike many other common trace minerals, can be toxic in sustained daily doses of 700 to 1,000 micrograms, so doctors urge caution in its use as part of your anti-aging regimen. The Food and Drug Administration has not established a recommended daily allowance for selenium, though a daily dose between 50 and 200 micrograms is considered safe and effective. As a precaution, women should avoid taking high doses of selenium during pregnancy or while breastfeeding.

Appendix A

More Sources of
Information

Books

Age-Proof Your Body: Your Complete Guide to Lifelong Vitality, by Elizabeth Somer, M.A., R.D. (Quill, 1999).

The Anti-Aging Plan: The Nutrient-Rich, Low-Calorie Way of Eating for a Longer Life, by Roy L. Walford and Lisa Walford (Marlowe & Company, 2005).

Gary Null's Ultimate Anti-Aging Program, by Gary Null, Ph.D. (Kensington, 1999).

Healthy Aging: A Lifelong Guide to Your Physical and Spiritual Well-Being, by Dr. Andrew Weil (Knopf, 2005).

Live Now, Age Later: Proven Ways to Slow Down the Clock, by Isadore Rosenfeld, M.D. (Warner Books, 1999).

The Longevity Bible: 8 Essential Strategies for Keeping Your Mind Sharp and Your Body Young, by Dr. Gary Small with Gigi Vorgan (Hyperion, 2006).

The New Anti-Aging Revolution, by Dr. Ronald Katz and Dr. Ronald Goldman, (Basic Health Publications, 2003).

The RealAge Makeover: Take Years off Your Looks and Add Them to Your Life, by Dr. Michael F. Roizen (Collins, 2004).

The Schwarzbein Principle II: The Transition— A Regeneration Program to Prevent and Reverse

Accelerated Aging, by Dr. Diana Schwarzbein with Marilyn Brown (HCI, 2002).

Successful Aging, by John W. Rowe, M.D., and Robert L. Kahn, Ph.D. (Dell, 1999).

Younger Next Year: A Guide to Living Like 50 Until You're 80 and Beyond, by Chris Crowley and Dr. Henry S. Lodge (Workman Publishing, 2004).

Web Sites

Ageless Design (offers informative monthly newsletter for Alzheimer's patients and caregivers)
www.agelessdesign.com

American Academy of Anti-Aging Medicine
www.worldhealth.net

Anti-Aging Lifestyle, Anti-Aging Therapy, Anti-Aging Medicine, Anti-Aging Science
www.anti-age.com

International Academy of Alternative and Anti-Aging Medicine
www.gvi.com/givweb/iaam

Rx for Wellness
www.rxforwellness.com

Appendix B

Organizations and Associations

Health

Administration on Aging
330 Independence Avenue SW
Washington, DC 20201.
Tel: 202-619-0724
www.aoa.gov

Aging Network Services
4400 East-West Highway
Bethesda, MD 20814
Tel: 301-657-4329
www.agingnets.com

Alzheimer's Association
919 North Michigan
Chicago, IL 60611
Tel: 800-272-3900
www.alz.org

American Academy of Dermatology
930 North Meacham Road
P.O. Box 4014
Schaumberg, IL 60168-4014
Tel: 847-330-0230
www.aad.org

American Academy of Ophthalmology
P.O. Box 7424
San Francisco, CA 94120-7424
Tel: 800-684-9788
www.aao.org

American Association of Cardiovascular and Pulmonary Rehabilitation
7611 Elmwood Avenue,
Suite 201
Middleton, WI 53562
Tel: 608-831-6989
www.aacvpr.org

American Association of Retired Persons (AARP)
601 E Street NW
Washington, DC 20049
Tel: 202-434-2277
www.aarp.org

American Cancer Society, Inc.
National Headquarters
1599 Clifton Road NE
Atlanta, GA 30329-4251
Tel: 404-320-3333
For the number of your local Cancer Society,
call 800-227-2345
www.cancer.org

American College of Sports Medicine
P.O. Box 1440
Indianapolis, IN 46206
Tel: 317-637-9200
www.acsm.org

American Diabetes Association
1660 Duke Street
Alexandria, VA 22314
Tel: 800-DIABETES (342-2383)
www.diabetes.org

American Dietetic Association
216 West Jackson Boulevard, Suite 800
Chicago, IL 60606
Tel: 800-366-1655 (Nutrition Hotline)
www.eatright.org

American Psychological Association
750 First Street NE
Washington, DC 20002
Tel: 202-336-5500
www.apa.org

American Sleep Disorders Association
1610 14th Street NW
Rochester, MN 55901
Tel: 507-287-6006
www.aasmnet.org

American Society of Plastic Surgeons
444 East Algonquin Road
Arlington Heights, IL 60005
Tel: 888-475-2742
www.plasticsurgery.org

Anxiety Disorders Association of America
Dept. B, P.O. Box 96505
Washington, DC 20077-7140
Tel: 301-231-9350
www.adaa.org

Arthritis Foundation
1314 Spring Street
Atlanta, GA 30309
P.O. Box 19000
Atlanta, GA 30326
Tel: 800-283-7800
www.arthritis.org

American Heart Association
7272 Greenville Avenue
Dallas, TX 75231-4596
Tel: 214-373-6300
For the number of your local Heart Association, call 800-AHA-USA1 (242-8721)
www.americanheart.org

American Institute for Cancer Research
1759 R Street NW
Washington, DC 20009
Tel: 800-843-8114
www.aicr.org

Center for Mind/Body Medicine
5225 Connecticut Avenue NW, Suite 414
Washington, DC 20015
Tel: 202-966-7338
www.cmbm.org

Council for Responsible Nutrition
1300 19th Street NW, Suite 310
Washington, DC 20036
Tel: 202-872-1488
www.crnusa.org

Food and Drug Administration
5600 Fishers Lane
Rockville, MD 20857-0001
Tel: 888-463-6332
www.fda.gov

International Academy of Alternative Health and Medicine
218 Avenue B
Redondo Beach, CA 90277
Tel: 310-540-0564
www.grg.org

International Federation on Aging
601 E Street NW
Washington, DC 20049
Tel: 202-434-2427
www.ifa-fiv.org

National Association of Area Agencies on Aging
1730 Rhode Island Avenue NW
Washington, DC 20036
Tel: 202-872-0888
www.n4a.org

National Council on Aging
409 Third Street SW, Suite 200
Washington, DC 20024
Tel: 800-424-9046
www.ncoa.org

National Eye Institute
Information Office, Building 31, Room 6A32
31 Center Drive MSC 2510
Bethesda, MD 20892-2510
Tel: 301-496-5248
www.nei.nih.gov

National Health Information Center
P.O. Box 1133
Washington, DC 20013
Tel: 301-565-4167
www.health.gov

National Heart, Lung, and Blood Institute Information Center
P.O. Box 30105
Bethesda, MD 20824-0105
Tel: 301-251-1222
www.nhlbi.nih.gov

National Hypertension Association
324 East 30th Street
New York, NY 10016
Tel: 212-889-3557
www.nathypertension.org

National Institute on Aging's Alzheimer's Disease Education and Referral Center
P.O. Box 8250
Silver Spring, MD 20907-8250
Tel: 800-438-4380
www.nia.nih.gov/Alzheimers

**National Institutes of Health
National Institute on Aging
Information Center**
P.O. Box 8057
Gaithersburg, MD 20898-8057
Tel: 800-222-2225
(Publication Info)
or 301-496-1752 (Information Center)
www.nih.gov

National Institute of Mental Health
5600 Fishers Lane, Room 7C-02
Rockville, MD 20857
Tel: 301-443-4513
www.nimh.nih.gov

National Institute of Neurological Disorders and Stroke
31 Center Drive, MSC 2540
Bethesda, MD 20892-2540
Tel: 800-352-9424
www.ninds.nih.gov

National Kidney and Urologic Diseases Information Clearinghouse
3 Information Way
Bethesda, MD 20892-3560
Tel: 301-654-4415
http://kidney.niddk.nih.gov

National Osteoporosis Foundation
1150 17th Street NW,
Suite 500
Washington, DC 20036-4603
Tel: 202-223-2226
www.nof.org

National Parkinson Foundation
1501 NW 9th Avenue
Miami, FL 33136
Tel: 800-327-4545
www.parkinson.org

National Women's Health Information Center
Tel: 800-994-9662
www.4woman.gov

National Women's Health Network
514 10th Street NW, Suite 400
Washington, DC 20004
Tel: 202-347-1140
www.nwhn.org

North American Menopause Society
P.O. Box 94527
Cleveland, OH 44101-4527
Tel: 440-442-7550
www.menopause.org

Older Women's League (OWL)
666 11th Street NW,
Suite 700
Washington, DC 20001
Tel: 202-783-6686
www.owl-national.org

National Institute of Arthritis and Musculoskeletal and Skin Diseases / Osteoporosis and Related Bone Diseases National Resource Center
1150 17th Street NW, Suite 500
Washington, DC 20036-4603
Tel: 800-624-BONE (2663)
www.osteo.org

President's Council on Physical Fitness and Sports
200 Independence Avenue SW, Room 738-H
Washington DC 20201
Tel: 202-690-9000
www.fitness.gov

Skin Cancer Foundation
245 Fifth Avenue, Suite 1403 NW
New York, NY 10016
Tel: 800-SKIN-490 (754-6490)
www.skincancer.org

Aging Research

Academy of Pharmaceutical Research and Science
2215 Constitution Avenue NW
Washington, DC 20037
Tel: 202-628-4410
www.aphanet.org

Aeron Lifecycles
1933 Davis Street, Suite 310
San Leandro, CA 94577
Tel: 800-631-7900
www.aeron.com

Alcor Life Extension Foundation
7895 East Acoma Drive, Suite 110
Scottsdale, AZ 85260-6916
Tel: 877-462-5267
www.alcor.org

Alliance for Aging Research
2021 K Street NW, Suite 304
Washington, DC 20006
Tel: 202-293-2856
www.agingresearch.org

American Academy of Anti-aging Medicine
1341 West Fullerton Avenue, Suite 111
Chicago, IL 60614
Tel: 773-528-1000
www.worldhealth.net

American Federation for Aging Research
1414 Avenue of the Americas, 18th Floor
New York, NY 10019
Tel: 212-752-2327
www.afar.org

American Geriatrics Society, Inc.
770 Lexington Avenue, Suite 300

New York, NY 10021
Tel: 212-308-1414
www.americangeriatrics.org

American Society of Human Genetics
9650 Rockville Pike
Bethesda, MD 20814
Tel: 301-571-1825
www.faseb.org/genetics

Bio Research Institute
4492 Camino de la Plaza,
Suite TIJ-1063
San Diego, CA 92173-3097
Tel: 800-291-1508
www.7hz.com

Dana Alliance for Brain Initiatives
745 Fifth Avenue, Suite 700
New York, NY 10151
Tel: 212-223-4040
www.dana.org

Division on Aging
Harvard Medical School
643 Huntington Avenue
Boston, MA 02115
Tel: 617-432-1840

Harvard Health Letter
154 Longwood Avenue
Boston, MA 02115
Tel: 617-432-1485
www.health.harvard.edu

Life Extension Foundation
P.O. Box 229120
Hollywood, CA 33022

Tel: 800-841-5433
www.lef.org

National Foundation for Brain Research
1250 24th Street NW, Suite 300
Washington, DC 20037
Tel: 202-293-5453

Index

A

Aging, 19–34
    emotional effects of, 27–29
    gender and, 22
    mental acuity with, 29–34
    physiology of, 20–25
    psychological effects of,
        26–27
Air pollution, 109–16
    reducing in home, 113–16
    sources, 111–12
Antioxidants, 166–69
Arthritis, 64, 90–91, 100
Associations/organizations,
    204–9

B

Bone density, 23–24. *See also*
    Osteoporosis
Books, 200–201
Brain changes, 22

C

Caffeine, 75
Calcium, 47–48, 99, 146–48
Caloric restriction approach,
    169–73
Cancer
    environmental factors,
        98–99, 102
    melatonin and, 185, 187
    nutrition and, 39, 66, 89–90
    selenium and, 194–95

Changes, with age, 20–25
Charity/volunteer work, 124–
    25, 126–27
Checkups, 12–14, 73
Chromium, 188–90

D

Dementia, 30, 87
Depression, beating, 75–77
DHEA supplementation, 155–
    56, 176–78
Diabetes, 93–94, 100
Diet. *See* Nutrition
Differently abled, 161–63
    Diseases, age-related, 85–
        100. *See also* Cancer
    arthritis, 64, 90–91, 100
    common, 86–94
    dementia, 30, 87
    diabetes, 93–94, 100
    genetics/family history and,
        16, 95–97
    heart disease, 87–88, 97–98,
        186, 195
    preventing, 97–100. *See also*
        Regimen, anti-aging
    stroke, 86, 195
Doctor
    checkup content/frequency,
        12–14, 73
    choosing, what to look for,
        5–10

finding common ground,
6–7
getting recommendations
for, 10
qualifying questions for,
10–11
your needs for, 7–8

E
Emotions
aging affecting, 27–29
depression and, 75–77
Environment, 101–16. *See
also* Air pollution
cancer and, 98–99, 102
common hazards of, 103–6
longevity and, 102–3
routes of exposure, 105–6
water pollution, 106–9
Exercise
becoming difficult, 21
differently abled and, 163
importance/benefits of,
36–38, 73
longevity and, 38–39
men and, 139–41
stress reduction with, 73
types of, 36–37

F
Family support, 17, 119–21
Friends, 122–26
benefits of friendship,
122–23
expanding circle of, 124–25
in old age, 127–31
positive attitudes and, 129

role of/support from, 17,
122–24
staying in touch with,
125–26

G
Gender differences. *See also*
Men; Women
life expectancy, 143–46
minerals, 147–51
Osteoporosis and, 91, 92,
147
recognizing, 134–36
Genetics and family history, 16,
95–97
Goals, 15

H
Hair changes, 21–22
Hearing loss, 23, 24
Heart changes, 20–21
Heart disease, 87–88, 97–98,
186, 195
Herbal remedies, 53–68
anti-aging regimen and,
54–55
for common ailments,
63–66
garlic, 65–66
obtaining, 66–68
precautions, 58–63, 152
side effects, 62–63
simplicity of, 57–58
testing medical use of,
55–57
High blood pressure, 71, 88, 98

Hormones. *See* Natural hormone approach
Human growth hormone, 155, 156–58, 173–76

I

Immortality, quest for, 2–5
Iron, 48, 148–50

L

Life expectancy
    gender differences, 143–46
    limits of, 3–4
Lifestyle
    matching to age, 158–61
    men and, 141–43
Lung elasticity, 21

M

Magnesium, 49, 190–93
Melatonin, 182–87
Memory. *See* Mental acuity
Men
    anti-aging and, 136–43
    balding, 22
    exercise and, 139–41
    lifestyle and, 141–43
    recognizing differences
        between women and,
        134–36
    sexual function changes, 25,
        82–83
    testosterone levels/aging
        and, 152, 178–81
Menopause, 25, 147–48, 152–53
Mental acuity

dementia and, 30, 87
exercises for, 32–34
maintaining, 29–34
Metabolic changes, 20, 36
Minerals, 47–51, 146–51, 152,
    187–97. *See also* Vitamins
    calcium, 47–48, 99, 146–48
    chromium, 188–90
    iron, 48, 148–50
    magnesium, 49, 190–93
    phosphorous, 49–50
    potassium, 50–51
    selenium, 51, 193–97
    zinc, 150–51

N

Natural hormone approach,
    173–87
    DHEA, 155–56, 176–78
    human growth hormone,
        155, 156–58, 173–76
    melatonin, 182–87
    testosterone, 151–52, 155–56, 178–81
Nutrition
    antioxidants and, 166–69
    caloric restriction and,
        169–73
    dietary guidelines, 41,
        159–61
    food reacting with medica-
        tions, 162–63
    good vs. bad foods, 40–41
    men and, 137–39
    minerals, 47–51, 146–51,
        152

preventing disease with, 39,
97–100
role of, 39–40
in senior years, 159–61
vitamins, 42–47, 152

O
Obesity, 100
Organizations/associations,
204–9
Osteoporosis, 24, 91–92, 99–
100, 147

P
Phosphorous, 49–50
Physiological changes, 20–25
Pineal gland, aging and, 182–
84
Plan, customizing, 5, 14–17,
135–36
Population differences. *See* Gen-
der differences; Men; Senior
population; Women
Potassium, 50–51
Pregnancy/childbearing   and
aging, 153–54
Psychological effects, of aging,
26–27

R
Regimen, anti-aging
customizing plan, 5, 14–17,
135–36
herbs and, 54–55
importance of, 4
Resources, 200–209

S
Selenium, 51, 193–97
Senior population
anti-aging and, 154–58
diet and, 159–61
hormonal enhancements for,
155–58
support systems for, 123–24,
127–31
Sensory changes, 22–23
Sex
aging and, 24–25, 81–84
bodily function changes
and, 25, 82–83
longevity and, 78–81
working with partner on,
78–81
Sleep, 73, 186
Smoking, 97–98, 114
Social support systems, 117–31
charity/volunteerism, 124–
25, 126–27
family, 17, 119–21
friends, 17, 122–26
health benefits of, 118–19
in old age, 123–24, 127–31
professional help, 121
Spiritual development, 125
Stress
effects of, 70–72
reducing, 72–75. *See also*
Social support systems
Stroke, 86, 195

T

Testosterone, 25, 151–52, 155–56, 178–81

U

Urinary tract changes, 24

V

Vision changes, 23

Vitamins, 42–47, 152. *See also* Minerals

Volunteer work, 124–25, 126–27

W

Water pollution, 106–9

Web sites, 201

Women

anti-aging and, 143–46

anti-aging supplementation and, 151–53

menopause and, 25, 147–48, 152–53

nutrition for, 146–51

Osteoporosis and, 24, 91–92, 99–100

pregnancy/childbearing and aging, 153–54

recognizing differences between men and, 134–36

sexual function changes, 82–83

Z

Zinc, 150–51